ALLIED
DUNBAR

MONEY GUIDES

GW00367078

YOUR HOME
IN FRANCE

ALLIED DUNBAR

MONEY GUIDES

YOUR HOME IN FRANCE

HENRY DYSON

LONGMAN

© Allied Dunbar Financial Services Limited 1989

ISBN 0-85121-520-3

Published by

Longman Law, Tax and Finance
Longman Group UK Limited
21-27 Lamb's Conduit Street, London WC1N 3NJ

Associated Offices

Australia, Hong Kong, Malaysia, Singapore, USA

A CIP catalogue record for this book is available from the British Library.

Printed and bound in Great Britain by
Biddles Ltd, Guildford and King's Lynn

Every care has been taken in preparing this book. The guidance it contains is sound at the time of publication but it is not intended to be a substitute for skilled professional assistance except in the most straightforward situations. You are also advised that the law in France can and does change quite frequently and it would not be unusual to find individual variations in the different regions and *départements*.

Because of this, the author, the publishers and Allied Dunbar Financial Services Ltd (or any other company within the Allied Dunbar Group) can take no responsibility for the outcome of action taken or not taken as a result of reading this book.

Contents

Foreword

I am delighted to have been given the opportunity by Allied
Dunbar and Longman publishers through the medium of this
book to do my best to help its readers avoid the major pitfalls
of buying and building property in France so that they may
become happy, trouble-free owners. However, there is much
more to reaping the full benefit of home ownership in
France, whether it is of a holiday home or of a home in
which you live permanently, than avoiding legal pitfalls. You
must get to know the French. It is a waste of time and
money to buy property in another country and not make
some effort to learn its language and understand its people.
You must learn how to enjoy all that is best in France of
which there is much and how to deal with its less attractive
aspects, since France, like every other country, is not exempt
from certain character defects.

Living in France by Philip Holland which is published by
Robert Hale will in this respect provide an admirable
companion to this book. Not only does it cover subjects of
which you will need to know more if you decide to buy in
France and which are outside the scope of this book but it
attempts also to give an insight into why the French behave
in the way in which they do. It should therefore help you to
extract the maximum pleasure from your home in France.
The quotation from Philip Holland's book at the beginning of
Chapter 15 appears with the permission of its author and
publishers.

1 Introduction

The problems which face the British buyer of property in
France are quite different from those which confront buyers
of property, for example, in the Iberian Peninsula. France is
not a country where property development has taken place
specifically with a view to attracting the foreigner although
his money is as welcome as that of any other buyer. There
are no ghettos where each nationality lives in blocks of flats
built by a developer of the same nationality, surrounded by
shops and restaurants which depend for their custom on the
flat-owners who require to eat the type of food they eat at
home and drink the drink imported into the UK and then re-
exported with a safe English label into the country from
which it came.

If there are problems of property frauds, which today can
still frighten the English buyer of property abroad, in France
these are almost certainly problems in which the buyer has
himself knowingly participated in an effort to save himself
money. These include cash payments to avoid French VAT
and the deliberate insertion of false prices in documents to
reduce stamp duties and in both cases it takes two to play the
game. Almost all problems stem from not taking proper
advice about a legal system which is considerably different
from the English system.

What this book is all about

The intention of this book is to explain how property —
houses, flats or land — is bought in France. No one should

contemplate buying property without knowing exactly why they want to do this and, therefore, what it is they should buy. You should remember that the house market is not a 'tourist' market and that estate agents in France tend to be very localised in the properties they have on their books. However, buying through agencies or at exhibitions in the UK is not necessarily the best way. What you must also remember (but without in the least being discouraged) is that you are buying a home in a foreign country and so:

- the contract you will be asked to sign will be not only in French but in legal French and it may be one of a number of different types of contracts, and all other documents involved will be in similar French
- the French legal system is wholly different from the English legal system
- the French tax system is different from the English tax system.

There is no reason to expect that you know any of the rules but there is every reason to hope that you will take expert advice about these rules for which, of course, you must be prepared to pay. You would not try to buy a house in England without the services of a solicitor and to attempt to do so abroad without similar assistance is not only foolhardy but, in the case of purchases in France, can, as you will read later on, be a grave disservice to your family.

Be prepared to seek advice

You have taken the first step; you have bought this book. The question is where do you go now for the kind of advice you will need to make certain that the pitfalls are avoided? What must you do to make certain that your purchase is not only properly dealt with from a French legal point of view but takes into account, if it is of a holiday home, that you are still living in England or, if it is a retirement home, of your British nationality and background. Ideally, the person to advise you is someone with a considerable knowledge of and practical experience in both English and French law who preferably lives in France. It may be that your own solicitor has such a contact but one of the best alternative sources of information is either the local British Consul or the manager of one of the local 'British' banks. Either of these will know the person they recommend and the extent of their experience. This is of considerable importance because in all probability you will be advised to give that person a power of attorney to act for you on completion and generally to look after your interests.

A word of warning

French consumer protection law covers a wide variety of situations and much of it relating to property purchases and building goes back a number of years. The French legal system is incredibly slow: often it will take two years for a case to get to court and about 50% of all cases go to appeal, taking at least another two years. In theory, there is likely to be a rule or regulation available to deal with most of what could go wrong in the majority of cases. The difficulty is that theory is not practice. The moral is, if you cannot avoid every problem, at least avoid as many as you can by taking the right advice from the right person from the very beginning.

This book is intended to help you by taking a look at the matters you should bear in mind when you are about to become involved in property transactions in France. It is written in general terms and so is not meant to take the place of specific advice about a particular situation. Do not treat it as a DIY guide to buying and selling French property. It is hoped that it will be of general interest and help you to avoid the pitfalls and understand the advice which you have wisely sought.

2 Where to buy

The climate

Paris is taken to be the norm when discussing the climate in France and this is about the same as the climate in London. You have to go at least as far south as the Loire to find a gentler climate, which tends to be wetter in the west and drier in the east. An exception to this is a small part of Normandy around Dieppe and Brittany which enjoys a climate very similar to parts of southern Cornwall or the west of Ireland, ie it is mild but extremely rainy.

The area to the east of Bordeaux — Bergerac and the Dordogne which are very popular with the British — has long warm summers but is rainy and foggy in winter. Further south along the Atlantic coast, in the south-west corner of France, the weather is warmer in summer but just as wet in winter, with a cold Atlantic Ocean to bathe in.

The Massif Central acts as a barrier between north and south so that, south of this mountainous range, there are long hot summers and short wet winters. The mistral, a cold gap wind, blows down the Rhone valley affecting the whole of southern and western Provence and the Tramontane blows in the Rousillon-Longuedoc region. Except for the area between Narbonne and Montpellier, where they can be very fierce, these winds are a minor irritant but should be taken into account. Finally, there is the area known as the Midi, stretching from the Pyrenees to the Alps (which includes the Rousillon-Longuedoc, a part of Provence and all the Côte d'Azur) which is hot and dry except for a couple of months in early spring when the annual rains fall, sometimes heavily.

What to buy

There is a wide range of properties available, whose prices vary enormously depending not only on the kind of property involved but the area in which it is situated. There is land available for building whatever house the planners will allow you to build and there are building estates run as condominiums where either you buy a plot of land and build or have built for you a house in accordance with whatever overall planning consent has been obtained for the estate. There are new houses and old houses, town houses and village houses. There are new flats and old flats. There are *mas* and there are *châteaux* – dilapidated and ripe for renovation or already restored. There is no limit to what is available but each kind of property has its own special attractions and problems. Building land is dealt with in Chapter 6.

When it comes to existing houses and flats, you must be careful with the meaning of the word 'new'. New tends to mean either that a property is brand new and you will be the first owner or that it has been completed within the last five years and the sale to you would qualify for a reduced rate of stamp duty (see Chapter 8). It is customary for estate agents to refer to a sale of property to a buyer who is not the first owner as a *revente* but this does not mean that you will not benefit from low stamp duty.

Flats have a vocabulary of their own. *Grand luxe* and 'grand standing' are similar to 'luxury' or 'high class' in England. *Vue imprenable* is intended to suggest a view (of the sea, mountains etc) which will endure for ever. In fact, it means that the existing view is clear of obstruction but promises nothing as to the future. Flats built some years ago in the turn-of-the-century style with high ceilings, large rooms and vast windows are known as *bourgeois* or 'monied class'. Unless they have been modernised, they will have fairly undesirable bathrooms and kitchens and probably any room which is not a 'public' room will be dowdy. This is because the French — and particularly the French bourgeoisie — are very anxious to make a good impression on visitors at the expense of what the visitors do not see. These flats have a certain charm but will be expensive to decorate, furnish and upkeep.

More modern flats have smaller rooms but the standard of building will certainly be less high than with older flats. The most modern will have individual heating and hot water. Avoid those that do not since you will find that your service charges will include the cost of heating other people's flats and providing other people with hot water. Do not worry too much about stamp duty being low on very new flats and high on older flats. On the whole, the fact that stamp duty is low on new flats tempts developers to charge buyers that bit more than they otherwise could. Modern flats are available from a studio design to those with five rooms. Remember that the French describe flats by the number of rooms and not by the number of bedrooms and that prices increase the higher it is situated in a block.

The *mas* is a farmhouse in the south and south-west of France. There is a certain chic about owning one. Indeed, they are sought-after and relatively expensive. It is not easy to find one for restoration but they do exist. Not only will you need expert architectural help but also builders and other tradesmen whom you can trust to begin, carry on and finish the work. The average *mas* is exactly where you would expect a farm to be and hence can be very unpleasant in winter if there are holes in the walls, no central heating and ill-fitting windows because your builders have failed to keep to their completion date.

A *château* can be anything from a real Loire castle to a large country house in good, poor or dilapidated condition. They are to be found all over France and the genuine ones are

those which are in the right style for the place where they are
built. Among the most attractive but, alas, rare are the
gentilhommières to be found throughout the country other
than Provence and principally in Languedoc and the Ile de
France. These are small 18th-century houses built for the
gentry and usually have some six to eight bedrooms and
numerous rooms on the ground floor.

Prices vary according to the part of the country where the
property is and the condition in which it is in. As with the
English manor or court house, anything fashionable or
sought-after is expensive. Beware the tumbledown farmhouse
and the property 'suitable for restoration'; it is likely to be
offered at a price which is unreasonable in France even if it
seems cheap by current English standards. Anything really of
interest will, apart from being expensive, possibly carry with
it the problem of being a listed building since the French
control these both indoors as well as outdoors.

Where to buy

Côte d'Azur

For well over 100 years the Côte d'Azur has been the happy
hunting ground for the British buyer. It stretches from
Menton to La Napoule but the area has been extended
westward to include St Tropez as more and more villages on
the coast have been developed. Along the coast as far as
Marseilles is a series of resorts and villages, many with
marinas, which are particularly attractive to yachtsmen. They
vary considerably in price and quality: of those to the east of
Nice, Cap Ferrat, Beaulieu and Villefranche are probably the
most attractive and expensive. Nice and Cannes are certainly
not cheap either, but Cannes is the more expensive.

Provence

Parallel to the coast but some miles inland is a string of Provençal villages, some of which are particularly attractive and some of which have suffered from the tourist trade. In this area are also 'two season' villages and small towns, equally attractive in summer and available for skiing in winter. The motorway from Aix en Provence to the frontier at Menton runs parallel to the coast on average 10 to 15 miles away until, close to Cannes, it comes almost down to the sea. The Var, which is the *département* through which it passes before reaching Cannes, is a delightful area and it is well worth while thinking of land for building between the motorway and the coast as well as north of the motorway into deep country.

The area between Toulouse and the Gulf of Lion contains the wine lake of France. Hot and dry in summer, the coastal area in the Rousillon-Longuedoc has special charm. Property prices here are much lower than on the Côte d'Azur and they tend to drop the further north you go.

The Dordogne

Further north along the Atlantic coast is Bordeaux which is considerably less hot than the south of France and is where the airport for the Dordogne is situated. It has a charm of its own, delicious food and quite interesting wines.

Normandy

Currently, interest seems centred on the more northern parts of France which are said to be within easy reach of the mouth of the Channel Tunnel. Property prices in these areas are for the moment lower than those in some other parts of the country.

Source: French Government Tourist Office

When to house-hunt

Two weeks' holiday is not enough to judge whether you will like a particular area or property. It is vital to see your chosen area of purchase at all times of the year but especially in high summer and mid-winter. A great number of northern Europeans find they cannot take the full brunt of a Mediterranean summer and cannot cope with shopping and household chores in the heat. For these people the more central or westerly parts of France would be the answer. Spring and autumn are delightful seasons throughout France but, at higher altitudes, spring can arrive relatively late and autumn can start surprisingly early, often in the second week of September.

Those purchasing flats where the block has a pool would do well to estimate in advance how many people could be using the pool in high summer. What looks charming and large in April can turn out to be pathetically inadequate in August. You will, of course, want your house guests to be able to use the pool, as will all the other *co-propriétaires* and it needs little imagination to realise how very crowded the pool area can become.

How to get there

France has many airports into which fly both international and national airlines. There are direct flights from various airports in the UK to destinations all over France and there is a continuous shuttle service from Heathrow to Paris. Charter flights to certain airports abound during the tourist season but fares from the UK may seem unreasonably high. The airport at Marseilles is not often offered as a suitable place to use but it is far more convenient than Nice Airport for the western end of the south coast. The airports at Montpellier, Toulouse, and Lyons may not regularly be served direct from the UK and may not benefit from charter flights but by using them you may save yourself time, since they can easily be reached via Paris.

Road travel in France presents very few problems. There is a vast network of motorways and a well-maintained system of main and secondary roads. More and more motorways are being built and much of France is now, in normal conditions, within an easy day's drive from Paris. Remember, however, that all traffic from the north of Europe to Spain and Portugal passes through France, as does traffic on its way to parts of Italy. Therefore, at the height of the season, both in summer and in winter, traffic conditions can be very difficult on some of the motorways.

France also boasts an excellent railway system which enables you to put a car on a train and sleep through the night instead of driving from the Channel coast to the south and west. There are also a number of high-speed trains which cross the country remarkably quickly. On the whole, rail travel is not expensive and many special reductions are available.

There are, nevertheless, certain things worth remembering when travelling in France. As you would expect, all estate agents underestimate the time it takes to get from any point of arrival to the house they want to sell. You can discover the truth only by completing the journey yourself. There are also certain places which although they are quite close to airports or motorways can be, at the height of the tourist season, extremely tedious to reach because of the large number of people travelling in these areas. Getting to and from a holiday home is an important point, particularly if you have children, and, if you are setting up permanently in France, local communications are as important as they are in the UK.

No mention has been made of Monaco because it is not part of France. Becoming a resident in Monaco can have certain advantages but, except in rather special cases, if you plan to live there because of the tax savings, you are liable to find that the cost of living is such that what you hope to save on tax you will spend on cups of coffee. Monaco has its own rules and regulations with regard to property and virtually nothing of what you read in this book applies to that principality.

Code Numbers of French *Departments* (Counties)

01 — Ain
02 — Aisne
03 — Allier
04 — Alpes de Haute Provence
05 — Hautes-Alpes
06 — Alpes-Maritimes
07 — Ardèche
08 — Ardennes
09 — Ariège
10 — Aube
11 — Aude
12 — Aveyron
13 — Bouches-du-Rhône
14 — Calvados
15 — Cantal
16 — Charente
17 — Charente-Maritime
18 — Cher
19 — Corrèze
20 — Corse
21 — Côte-d'Or
22 — Côtes-du-Nord
23 — Creuse
24 — Dordogne
25 — Doubs
26 — Drôme
27 — Eure
28 — Eure-et-Loir
29 — Finistère
30 — Gard
31 — Haute-Garonne
32 — Gers
33 — Gironde
34 — Hérault
35 — Ille-et-Vilaine
36 — Indre
37 — Indre-et-Loire
38 — Isère
39 — Jura
40 — Landes
41 — Loir et Cher
42 — Loire
43 — Haute-Loire
44 — Loire-Atlantique
45 — Loiret
46 — Lot
47 — Lot-et-Garonne
48 — Lozère

49 — Maine-et-Loire
50 — Manche
51 — Marne
52 — Haute-Marne
53 — Mayenne
54 — Meurthe-et-Moselle
55 — Meuse
56 — Morbihan
57 — Moselle
58 — Nièvre
59 — Nord
60 — Oise
61 — Orne
62 — Pas-de-Calais
63 — Puy-de-Dôme
64 — Pyrénées Atlantiques
65 — Hautes-Pyrénées
66 — Pyrénées-Orientales
67 — Bas-Rhin
68 — Haut-Rhin
69 — Rhône
70 — Haute-Saône
71 — Saône-et-Loire
72 — Sarthe
73 — Savoie
74 — Haute-Savoie
75 — Paris
76 — Seine-Maritime
77 — Seine-et-Marne
78 — Yvelines
79 — Deux-Sèvres
80 — Somme
81 — Tarn
82 — Tarn-et-Garonne
83 — Var
84 — Vaucluse
85 — Vendée
86 — Vienne
87 — Haute-Vienne
88 — Vosges
89 — Yonne
90 — Territoire-de-Belfort
91 — Essonne
92 — Hauts-de-Seine
93 — Seine-Saint-Denis
94 — Val-de-Marne
95 — Val-d'Oise

CODE NUMBERS OF FRENCH "DEPARTEMENTS" (COUNTIES)

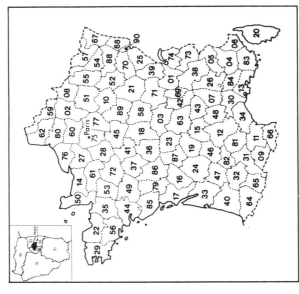

3 What to do and what not to do

This chapter discusses some points which you should bear in mind when you are buying property in France. The basic problem is that most English buyers of property in France are used to the English system where they have been guided through the trauma of house purchase by their solicitors. There is no equivalent to this service in France. The system expects you, in the majority of cases, to sign a contract prepared by an estate agent virtually without any previous enquiries and without the services of a surveyor. You are expected to make your own mortgage arrangements and also to sign a complicated purchase document in front of a notary who (quite properly) is often also acting for the seller. Finally, you will normally have to deal with the insurance of the property when you have bought it, when you are used to your solicitor doing this automatically for you.

Do not be put off in any way by all this. The solution is to entrust your purchase to a suitable adviser (preferably in France) who will look after your interests as far as possible as though you were buying in England.

Think of what you would do if you were buying property in the UK. You would:

- not necessarily buy the first house or flat you saw
- not sign a contract presented to you by the seller's agent but arrange for it to be sent to your solicitor
- work out carefully your financial situation and consult your bank manager or accountant or solicitor, to see if

you could afford the price asked and how you could best raise it
- if you were buying with a mortgage loan, get the offer of that loan before exchanging contracts or make the contract conditional on that offer
- if what you were buying was a 'second home', get your tax position clarified.

When you had decided that the house was what you were looking for and that you could afford it, you would go ahead in the knowledge that your solicitor would protect you from all legal problems.

Similar rules apply to buying property in France. However, the French cannot normally get all this advice from one person and have to do some of the work themselves. The solution is to treat yourself to the same sort of protection as you would in England. Added to this, there is the obvious problem that even if you speak French reasonably well, you probably do not speak legal and technical French. Therefore, you may find it difficult to negotiate and to get the kind of information you need to help you make decisions.

Remember that although fraudulent builders are rare, bankrupt builders are quite common. Do not sign building contracts given to you by builders without advice (would you do so in England?) and do not use architects recommended to you by builders. Let your chosen expert in France check out both architect and builder.

Watch your budget

You must bear in mind that buying (and selling) property in France can in many circumstances be more expensive than in the UK. Selling agents tend to charge approximately 5% commission although this may be hidden in the asking price in reality, it is the buyer who pays commission. On the other hand, whilst in limited circumstances new property carries a very reduced rate of stamp duty, a purchase outside this range will involve fees and disbursements of approximately 10%, of which stamp duty is a large proportion. Non-residents also have to pay capital gains tax, currently at the rate of 33.3%. Hence, changing houses can be expensive and it is worth while making the right choice first time round depending on your probable future plans: a holiday home that will always remain a holiday home, or something which can become a retirement home, or perhaps just a plot of land which can be built on in the future.

Never over-commit yourself. Wild fluctuations in the sterling/franc rate are rare but, as the minimum time between finding your property and completing will probably not be less than two months changes in the exchange rate are likely. If you are buying on 'plan' a flat or house which has not yet been completed, you will probably have to spread stage payments over at least a year. A turn against the franc could cause problems and you should get advice from your bank manager on how best to guard against this risk.

Remember that French legal costs and disbursements must be assumed to be about 10% of the purchase price. In certain cases, they can be much less but they could be higher and they *have* to be produced on or before completion. Do not rely on friends' estimations of costs: there are so many factors to take into account that there can be wide variations from purchase to purchase.

Remember also that if you have a French mortgage and your income to service it comes from the UK, you may have a long-term, two-country inflation problem to cope with as well as an exchange problem. The same applies for ordinary outgoings and, if you have bought a flat, for your service charges.

Look before you buy

It is a safe rule to rely upon in any country that the second
house you see is more suitable than the first. Do not be
'pushed' by selling agents; it is highly unlikely that you will
lose your 'dream' flat if you do not sign immediately. In any
case, no contract should be signed before you have taken
proper independent advice.

Although there appear to be no inspection flights to France,
it is often worth paying a second visit to the property you
think you will buy before making a final decision. If at this
stage you contact the right person in France for advice, they
will be able to 'keep warm' the property for you for a
reasonable period. If, after careful thought, you make your
decision to buy while you are in England, contracts can be
signed on your behalf without your returning to France.

Ideally, you should see the property that you are going to
buy in the worst possible conditions. It does rain even in the
south of France and during at least three months of the year
it can be chilly as well. If you are thinking of buying in the
north, make certain that the fact that the climate can be every
bit as unpleasant as in the UK has weighed sufficiently with
you. At least for the next few years, treat with reserve the
time schedules for Channel Tunnel travel. In the south of
France, every piece of property is said to be within a
maximum of 40 minutes of Nice Airport! It is probable that
the same convenient underestimate will be used by sellers
and their agents in the north. Best of all, if you are buying a
permanent home, it pays to spend a few months in France
just looking around. Why not rent a flat for a short while and
do this at your leisure?

The legal side

It is important to engage the services of the right kind of adviser in France. You will probably get the best advice from a suitably qualified English person living in France and with a knowledge of French law.

Do not sign anything without consulting the adviser you have chosen to look after your interests and never pay over money without his advice. If you feel that you must make some payment without being covered in this way, only make payments in favour of a notary.

If you are offered documents which have been translated into English to consider at your leisure, be extremely wary of what they say. Some will be in bad English but the most dangerous are those which are in reasonably good English but put French legal terms into what the translator thought were the equivalent English legal terms. Some results are amusing but others are terribly misleading.

A word on tax

You need not worry that all taxes due on the completion of a purchase in France will not be paid. It is the duty of the notary to see that this is done and he incurs jointly with you a personal liability to see that this happens. That is why he will never complete until he has in hand all the cash necessary to enable him to make these payments. Annual taxes in respect of French property are normally payable in arrears at the end of the year. You usually have about two months in which to pay, after which time 10% is added to the bill.

France is not a tax haven for people who cheat. Putting false values in documents for property will land you in trouble. Do not accept that it is safe or easy to do this; it is not true and the person who is trying to persuade you otherwise will almost certainly be the one who stands to benefit and you will be the one who stands to suffer.

4 The buying process

In France, as in England, buying property falls into two
parts: the contract and the conveyance. Essentially, in both
countries the object is to see that you get what you have
agreed to buy, that it brings with it no surprises, that it
serves the purpose for which it was sold to you and that you
get a good title to it. The way in which the French system
sets about this is rather different from how it is done in
England.

The contract

In England, when you have found the house you like, you
tell the estate agent to send details to your solicitor and you
pay him a visit. He gets in touch with the seller's solicitor
who sends him a draft of the contract. He then asks certain
questions and, when he is satisfied with all the answers and
with what the contract says, he explains it all to you and asks
you to sign it. The seller then signs his part of the contract
and the deal is done.

Not so in France. The normal procedure is for the seller's
estate agent to prepare the contract, which is often in
standard form, and to hand it to the buyer for his signature.
The buyer usually signs without question if the price is right
and the date for completion is satisfactory. In many cases, no
great harm is done by following this procedure if you are
buying a flat in one of the large cities, but if you are buying

land or any kind of property elsewhere, and *in particular in the country*, you should always get advice before signing anything. There are good reasons for this:

- There are a number of different kinds of document loosely called contracts. The most usual and satisfactory is the *compromis de vente* which, like the English contract, is signed by both parties and binds both parties from the moment of signature. There are also documents which you might reasonably think were binding contracts but which are nothing more than offers to sell or to buy and have no value at all until the offer has been accepted by the buyer or the seller, as the case may be. Even then, many contracts of this kind are void if not lodged for stamping (*enregistré*) within quite a short time. The type of contract used is partly a question of local usage and partly of what the selling agent normally uses or thinks he wants to use. Whilst it is not recommended that you sign even a straightforward *compromis de vente* without advice, you should *never* sign any other type of contract without getting advice.
- It is not unusual for agents to prepare contracts without having seen the seller's title deeds. This means that the property you are buying may be wrongly described and important details may be missing. This is bad enough with a flat in a block but in the case of country properties and land itself, this is dangerous. A full description should appear and, except in the simplest cases, insist on a cadastral plan.
- Watch out for deposits. Usually they are of the order of 10% and this is reasonable if completion is not delayed. Always pay deposits to your notary, or the seller's notary, and not to the estate agent. There are three types of deposit and what happens to them if either party defaults depends on which type they are. Usually, the contract will contain a penalty clause so that if the buyer defaults he will lose his deposit or the amount of the penalty if it is higher. If the seller defaults, he will pay the penalty amount. It is important to seek advice about this.
- Most contracts offered to you to sign give the name of the

notary who is to prepare the *acte de vente* and, in most cases, it will be the seller's notary. You must never accept this and insist on inserting the name of your own notary as well. This is your *absolute right*. You can instruct your own notary up to the day of completion, even if the contract contains only the name of the seller's notary. It is you who pays the notarial fee in any event and, if there are two notaries involved, they share a single fee.

- Watch out for the clause about commission, which is dealt with separately below.
- Some contracts provide for both parties to be liable for commission if the sale goes off by mutual agreement. This may seem surprising but so many French sellers try to avoid paying their agents' commission by conniving with the buyer to cancel the contract and then going quietly to the notary to complete the deal that it is hard not to advise the honest buyer to agree to this.
- It is rare for completion dates to be fixed but they are usually on an 'on or before' basis to allow time for searches and enquiries to be completed. This means that a deposit may be lying around for a long time when it could be retained by the buyer and earning interest. It is worth asking your bank to block the amount in a deposit account and to give a letter to the seller saying that it will irrevocably hand over the cash when it becomes due. Some banks will do this and some sellers will agree to it.
- Most searches are made after contracts have been signed so that contracts tend to be subject to rather general conditions that nothing untoward will turn up. Generally, property is sold subject to the condition that it is taken in the state it is on completion. Therefore, take note of anything that happens between contracts and completion.
- Every contract *must* contain a statement by the buyer to say whether he is buying with the aid of a loan or not (see below).
- If you are buying a flat in a condominium or a property on a *lotissement*, a copy of the *règlement de copropriété* should be made available with the contract *before* completion. It is also useful to have a copy of the last service charge account.

It is important to be aware of the fact that English law requires a contract for the sale of land to be in writing or to be evidenced by writing but that this is not so in France; it can be a verbal contract as long as it is clear exactly which property is to be sold and the sale price is agreed.

Seller's commission

The general rule in France is that the seller pays his selling agent's commission. This rule can, of course be varied by agreement between the parties. In certain parts of France, by tradition, either the commission is split between seller and buyer or it is paid by the buyer alone.

Unfortunately, it is not possible to say which these areas are since neither the estate agents nor the notaries outside these areas have any list of the places where these exceptions apply. On the whole, they are country areas in the south-west and west of the country, certain areas in the north and the whole of Alsace but this is not an exclusive list. The general rule applies throughout the south.

An additional difficulty is that in many places, it is the notaire and not an estate agent who negotiates the sale and in addition makes every effort to act also for the buyer ie prepares a contract which shows himself as the sole notary involved without advising the buyer of his right in this respect.

A further difficulty is that in a number of cases, the buyer will have instructed an agent in the UK to find him a property so that he may incur a 'finder's fee' and also the seller's commission and find that he has as notary the same person who not only acts for the seller but actually negotiated the sale from the seller to him.

All this is avoidable. There may in principle be no reason not to use the services of English estate agents when buying French property, but in practice this is not a course of action to be adopted without seeking the most careful legal advice from someone conversant with the practice in France. In any event *never sign any contract* in a purchase organised in this way without such advice.

House purchase loans

Every contract to buy a property must state whether the buyer is obtaining a loan to help towards the price. If he is, then the contract is automatically subject to the condition that he gets his loan and he is allowed a minimum of one month from the date of the contract to do so, although the period may be longer if the seller agrees. If he genuinely fails to obtain a loan, he may cancel the contract and will be reimbursed any money he has paid under it. It is obvious that no seller will agree to sell to a buyer who needs to get a loan which is unreasonably large or which the seller suspects that the buyer cannot obtain for one reason or another. It is no use for a buyer who wants to find an excuse to 'cry off' failing to look for a loan. Provided that it is on normal terms, the seller can find a loan for him and this will fulfil the condition. If a buyer states in the contract that he is not seeking a loan, he cannot at a later stage rely on this statutory condition.

Take note of the date of your contract: many contracts are signed on different dates by the seller and the buyer, but make certain that the contract is given the date of the last signature.

If you are thinking of buying jointly see Chapter 6.

The conveyance

The transfer of land in France is by an *acte de vente* or conveyance. Strictly speaking, a sale of land is complete between seller and buyer as soon as the contract is signed but it remains ineffective as against everyone else until registered at the *Bureau des Hypothéques*. Since for fiscal reasons only a notarial document can be so registered, the contract is 'repeated' in this form at completion. The *acte de vente* is usually a document many pages long, much of which is photocopied from the previous conveyance to the seller. This is one of the reasons why a buyer ought to use his own and not the seller's notary, for otherwise the same notary simply goes from one sale to another never rechecking the title since he first dealt with it.

It is pointless a buyer trying to go through an *acte de vente* in France. It will be quite beyond him. A buyer has therefore a number of choices: he lets the seller's notary act for him and takes a risk or he chooses his own notary but in either case he will probably not be given much explanation before or at completion and he may have difficulty in understanding much of what he is told. His third choice is to seek advice and appoint an adviser as his attorney, leaving it to him to vet everything and explain the procedure to him in his own language and in terms he can understand.

This last choice is ideal and really only coincides with what a buyer would be doing in England. If you appoint your own notary but do not take further advice, it is not so much that there is a risk of not getting good title to what you are buying; that you will probably get, but think of all the questions you ask your solicitor when you buy a home in England and all the advice you get from him. Would you be happy to do without that? There is no reason why you should deprive yourself of this valuable advice when you buy a home outside of England.

Completion

As a buyer attempting to deal with a purchase on your own, it is highly improbable that you will hear anything until you receive from the notary involved a letter giving you a date for completion. You will not, as in England, be advised from time to time of progress. The notary may assume that you are coming in person to complete or he may assume that you are appointing an attorney. The rule is that all parties to a notarial document must be present in person or represented by an attorney.

If you have asked a local adviser to act for you, he will keep you informed of the progress of purchase and, in due course, will send you a power of attorney. If you get a power of attorney directly from the notary, you would be wise not to use it. It will almost certainly appoint one of his clerks to be your attorney and this merely ensures that if all your requirements have not been complied with, or if there are any problems, there is no independent person to complain on your behalf. Also, your attorney, who should be acting in your interests alone, is an employee of the notary. Even at this late stage, if you have not sought advice before, seek it now. This does not mean that notaries cannot be trusted but that the French system of one notary for both parties is potentially dangerous, particularly if someone in his office is also acting as an attorney for you.

There are no exchange control rules about foreigners buying French property but it is not advisable to send cash needed for completion direct to the notary. Again, this is not because he cannot be trusted but because the cash will take a long time to arrive and on the the way will spend nights in various French banks earning interest for the French Government. Even when it arrives in the notary's account, it is in a special State bank where all notaries are obliged to have their clients' accounts and, if completion is delayed, it is M. le President de la Republique Française who is that much richer. It is preferable to open your own bank account so that the cash can stay on deposit there earning money for you until your local adviser, who will also be your attorney, is given a draft in favour of the notary on the day of actual completion.

The amount required on or before completion will include notarial fees, stamp duties and other disbursements. There is no 'completion statement' as there is in England. No problems arise on the registration of the conveyance to you as this is undertaken by your notary but usually there is no rush to do this. The registration procedure takes weeks or months depending on which local Land Registry is involved but it is not registration which perfects the transaction between you and the seller. It merely gives notice that you are now the owner of the property you have bought so that the tax authorities can collect *taxe foncière* or land tax from you.

In due course, you will receive the *expédition* or certified copy of your title document from your notary. Original title documents do not exist, that is to say, they are kept in the notary's records. There are no problems in France of properties which do not exist or non-existent title deeds such as have plagued buyers in Spain. There are sometimes problems about who owns a property because, unlike the English Land Registry, registration does not guarantee title. That is why you must have a notary separate from the seller's notary so that, when you buy, a single notary who investigates the title he offers to himself is not the only protection you have.

There are a number of local procedural variations in France. The procedure mentioned above is 'standard' but you must not be surprised if it does not follow exactly what you are asked to do.

5 Buying on plan

Buying 'on plan' or *en état futur d'achèvement* is a common way of buying flats in France. There is no reason why you should not buy a house in this way but since more flats than houses are being built, it is less common.

The advantages of this method of buying are that:

- you pay for your flat over a period of time rather than by one single payment, which may make things easier for you
- to some extent, it gives you the chance to choose interior decoration
- so far as the design of the building allows, you may also be able to change around the interior of your flat. Normally alterations of this kind will increase the price.

You will, of course, be told that you are buying tomorrow's flat at today's price but it seems improbable that the developer has not taken account of what tomorrow's price will be. You also suffer from the possible disadvantage that quite a large percentage of buildings are not completed on time.

The purchase contract

There is a very strict Law to protect people who buy in this way. The purchase contract is called, rather misleadingly for the British, a *contract de réservation*. This is not a reservation for you with the developer of a flat until you are ready to sign a contract to buy it but is itself a contract which binds you to buy. You will lose your deposit if you fail to complete. The contract must contain:

• a full description of the property to be sold plus outline specifications of the work which will be done. These should include references to domestic services to be supplied. The specifications are in fairly technical French or at least refer to types of French materials and equipment. Try to have these checked by an English surveyor or someone who can translate and explain
• the price together with a statement as to whether it is to be a firm price or subject to revision. Most prices are firm but if they can be varied, this must be in accordance with one of two indices, of which the Cost of Construction index is the more usual
• the time at which stage payments are to be made. These will be made on presentation of architect's certificates. The Law sets out what percentage of the price may be asked for at each stage. These are maximum payments and developers may (and often do) ask for more frequent and smaller payments but they must not ask for more than the legal maximum at any given stage
• the amount of the deposit (*réservation*). This may not exceed 5% if building is to be completed within one year or 2% if the delay is to be two years. Longer than that and no deposit may be taken. Deposits must be paid either to a notary or to a special blocked account with a bank.

Completion of the purchase as opposed to completion of the building works will be provided for in the contract. The Law requires that some of its clauses are repeated in the contract of which the most important are:

• you may ask for the return of your deposit if the developer does not sign the conveyance to you by the date mentioned in the contract

• you may also ask for the return of your deposit if on coming to complete you discover that the final price shown exceeds the price you were quoted by more than 5%. A deposit can also be reclaimed if a decrease in area or the quality of work on a property will reduce its value by more than 10% or if any of the domestic services proposed are to be omitted. Should this happen, there are formal rules as to how you get back your deposit and it is best to follow these strictly.

You are entitled to receive a draft of the conveyance a full month before completion and notaries for developers are fairly good about this. If you have instructed someone to advise you in France, do not hold on to these papers when they arrive but send them straight on to them otherwise the time available for investigation will be short.

The initial contract must also state what insurance or other guarantees the builder has obtained to cover proper completion of the building so that if you have paid some stage payments and something goes wrong you can get your money back.

What to do on the completion of building

In due course, when the building is completed, you will be asked to make the last stage payment, leaving 5% of the total price unpaid. At that stage, you are asked to inspect the property and confirm that all is in order and, if you find that it is, you hand over the balance of 5%. You are strongly advised to call in an expert to make this inspection for you. It is true that you have a right to call on the developer for a period of two years for small problems and for ten years in the case of major defects to put things right but there are obvious reasons why it is better to have these put right at the outset. A developer will react more positively to an expert's complaints in order to get his final 5% than to yours after he has had all he expects to get.

All these rules apply specifically to purchases on plan. They are in addition to the general rules on buying property dealt with in Chapter 4.

6 Building new property

Introduction

It is perhaps less easy to find suitable land on which to build a single house in France than in many other Mediterranean countries. This is because in the areas which are most popular with the British either almost all such land has already been bought — very often by developers for building estates — or it is agricultural land or/and designated as not available for building for other reasons under local planning schemes. Of course, there is building land available but it will be considerably easier to find in fairly remote areas where it may be difficult in the future to find a buyer for the house you have built. Remember that if you wish to sell your property, the buyer may well not be British. Since France is very much larger than the United Kingdom travelling distances are greater. 'Getting away from it all 'assumes for the French reasonable proximity to all those things which the British do not want to see for miles around when they make for their country cottage.

Some general thoughts

It must be a safe rule to follow — in France as elsewhere — that if land which looks very tempting is offered to you as building land in an area where such land is normally hard to come by, there is probably a very good reason why it has not been sold already.

There are still old houses available for restoration which in many cases amounts virtually to rebuilding. From a planning point of view, renovation or additions may well incur the same problems as new building so this chapter applies in large measure to acquisitions for both purposes.

In areas recognised as those where the visitor buys property, it is in the interests of planning authorities to foster building, provided it complies with normal planning exigencies. In other areas, where the tourist is not such a common sight, the French can be less welcoming towards the foreigner.

There is another very important distinction between buying land in or near developed areas and out in the country. French succession law keeps family property in the family and it is not rare to find land in the country owned in small proportions by a large number of members of one family. It can sometimes prove quite difficult to get all the co-owners to agree to sell, either because one or more of them is quite happy to blackmail gently as to the price or because some member of the family thinks it would be disloyal to part with a plot which has been owned by the family for generations. In towns and less remote parts of the country, developers have long ago discovered the technique for overcoming this problem.

Planning

Within the last few years, planning in France has been decentralised and is now dealt with at local level. This means not only that planning applications can be dealt with more speedily but also that a considerable amount of planning information can be obtained from the local *maire* and, in

the seller's lawyer but by an estate agent very often with
nothing more to go on than what the seller tells him. It is,
therefore, of the greatest importance when buying building
land not to sign anything without taking advice. Any contract
you do sign for the purchase of land should be conditional on
planning permission being obtained and if applicable, on
SAFER (a quasi-governmental agricultural committee which
oversees on a local basis the use of agricultural land) and
possibly on the local authority waiving their rights of
compulsory purchase. Unlike the situation in England, the
equivalent of local searches are not made before but after
exchange of contracts.

Building

From a practical point of view, there are four different
methods of getting a new house built. You can:

1   Buy the land with the house to be built on it from a
    developer using usually (but not necessarily) his plans.
    This is buying *en état futur d'achèvement* or 'on plan'.
    Special rules designed to protect buyers apply to this
    method (and also to buying a flat in a block which is still
    under construction) and are dealt with separately in
    Chapter 5.
    This method has the advantage of allowing you to pay by
    instalments as building progresses. Whilst you will not be
    able to alter your plans radically in midstream, it is
    usually possible to get the developer to make some
    changes although these may increase the agreed price.
2   If you already own land, you can get a professional
    builder to build you a 'one-off' house. He will normally
    offer a number of basic types but some variations can be
    made. He will undertake all the professional and technical
    work, in many cases subcontracting to various trades.
    Again, the law is strict in order to protect you. You are
    entitled to insist on a fixed price and to either a guarantee

from a bank or similar institution to ensure completion of the work or to pay by instalments only as work progresses. As you will see from the figures quoted below, much, if not all, depends on your choice of builder on which you must get prior advice.

3   Instead of using a professional builder, you can put your trust in an architect of your choice (but not of the estate agent acting for the seller of the land). The architect should be either someone who has proved their worth by working for trustworthy friends of yours or be recommended by a totally independent and qualified person. There are a very few English surveyors and architects working in France but finding one avoids the language problem. If you use a French architect, you must have a bilingual intermediary or you will inevitably have surprises. A recent survey has shown that to make use of an architect increases the overall cost of building (including his fees) by about 12%. Even with an architect watching over progress, the more often you put in an appearance on site the less should be the inevitable delays.

4   Finally, you can (but are not recommended to do so) with or without the help of an architect, make your own arrangements with local building trades. It gives you sole control over what is going on which is almost certainly just what you should not have.

Currently, method 1 is used for about 15% of the new houses built in France, method 2 for about 40%, method 3 for about 35% and method 4 for under 10%. The following figures may also help you to decide how you are going to set about building.

	Alterations to contracts	Price revisions	Delay in completion	Legal action needed	Bankruptcy of builder
Method 1	5%	5%	30%	5%	nil
Method 2 (top 10 firms)	23%	39%	16%	7%	nil
Method 2 (others)	22%	18%	34%	9%	13%
Methods 3 & 4	7%	10%	26%	5%	7%

If you decide to employ an architect and to entrust everything to him, you should discuss with him what you have in mind before you enter into any contract to buy the land. In this way, you should be able to ensure that your contract has all the necessary conditions in it so that if they are not fulfilled, you can 'cry off'.

What not to buy

There is of course land on the market which is unsuitable for building, waiting to be sold to the ill-advised or the unadvised. Among the reasons for land being unsuitable are:

• there is only a limited supply of water for household use
• there are geological problems often well known to the seller but not to you or anyone else not familiar with the area
• there are drainage problems
• local geographical problems such as sloping ground, prevailing winds, frost pockets and fog pockets.

All these matters should be borne in mind at pre-contract stage. Do not be overconcerned with steep slopes and rocks: good builders know how to deal with this. It is also a safe rule to be very suspicious of land for building sold to you by a builder.

For discussion with your architect

If the piece of land you have in mind fits the bill, remember also that the climate and way of doing things in France (particularly in the southern parts) can be very different from

those in England. Among the things useful to discuss with
your architect at an early stage are:

- the siting of the house. If you are in the south, you will
  probably spend a good deal of time outside. You may be
  yearning for the sun but after a time shade becomes
  important. Terraces and balconies should be placed
  accordingly
- discover what the prevailing wind is and take account of
  this when discussing siting
- space and how it is used are important for just as it is
  expensive to rectify oversights to a house so it is
  expensive to alter the interior. Is your holiday home going
  to become a permanent home? If so, it is perhaps better
  to have too many rooms in the beginning so as to have
  sufficient accommodation later on
- you will probably be required or at least strongly
  encouraged to build in local style. Do not resist this. A
  house which is not built with local materials in local style
  sticks out like a sore thumb
- consider very carefully all the methods of heating: gas, oil,
  electricity and solar. In the north of France and well
  down towards the south, you should think more or less in
  terms of an English winter. Even in the south, it can be
  chilly and damp in the winter months
- most houses in France have some kind of shutter. They
  are essential to keep out the heat in summer and the cold
  in winter
- modern French houses and flats do not lack light switches
  and electric points but they are often very oddly placed.
  You will have to insist on having yours where you want
  them. In general terms, the quality of electric fittings,
  plugs, switches etc leaves much to be desired. Although
  all modern buildings have circuit breakers rather than
  fuse boxes, French appliances tend to be un-earthed more
  often than in the UK. Outside plugs are very useful
- work surfaces tend to be lower than in the UK. A height
  of 92–94 cms is the norm in Britain
- if you are in the south and a keen gardener, see if you can

have an emergency water tank for use on lawns and plants if and when there is a shortage of water
- security is important, if not to you, at least to your insurance company. If you have a holiday home which is often left unoccupied, grills over the windows and a strong front door are essential
- parts of France become very hot in summer and very cold in winter. Proper insulation is therefore essential. Luckily, France is one of the most advanced countries in the world in this field. There are not only special plasterboards using glass-fibre and/or polystyrene but also special foam-filled partitions as well as architectural methods of creating internal air pressures to act as insulators. However, to take advantage of all this technology you must discuss the subject with your architect. If you find out too late that either your architect has not allowed for this kind of protection or that the builders have 'skimped' the work, it is very expensive to deal with insulation once the house is built.

This is not an exhaustive list and if you have a good architect, he should think of a lot more points. It does also help to seek advice from your neighbours. Do remember that too much which is out of the ordinary may be unreasonably expensive.

Your building contract is something you must not attempt to agree without specialist advice. This is even more important if the architect is the choice of the builder but, even if he is your choice, get the contract vetted by a lawyer before you sign it. The list of what can go wrong or provide you with surprises because you have failed to take advice is too long to set out here. You deserve all that can happen to you if you sign a building contract 'blind'.

7 You and French banks

Whether you are buying property in France for a permanent
or a holiday home, it is almost inevitable that you will need a
bank account in France or at least come into contact with the
French banking system. It is possible not to have a bank
account and to exist on Eurocheques and credit cards but you
will soon realise that this is impractical. On the other hand, it
is not a good idea to close your UK bank account or to throw
away your UK credit cards even if you are living in France
permanently. To maintain the former gives you a certain
freedom of action and to keep the latter avoids having to use
French credit cards which require you to pay off the whole
outstanding balance every month by direct debit from your
French bank account.

On the whole you will benefit from using the French branch
of your own bank in the UK. Three of the 'Big Four' have
branches in France which provide full banking facilities.
Although they are subject to French banking law, they are
familiar with English banking procedure and most of the
branches will have at least one member of the staff who is
English. In many cases, the manager or assistant manager
will also be English. This helps from a language point of view
because he can talk if necessary to your branch in the UK in
terms which they understand and, also, it facilitates the
transfer of cash between the two countries.

Exchange control in France has virtually disappeared and this
chapter therefore assumes that it no longer affects banking in
France. There are still some limits for large transactions
which may not be carried out without Banque de France

consent and the movement of more than 50,000 francs in cash (in any currency) over French frontiers should be reported to Customs. However, there are no restrictions on foreigners buying or selling property in France and no difficulties about getting the proceeds of sale of property out of France.

Bank accounts

The formalities for opening an account in France are similar to those in the UK. The bank will need a copy of your passport and a 'fiscal' address, that is, for the non-resident, your home in England, or for the resident, your home in France. On the whole, joint accounts have advantages, if only because on the death of one holder, the other can usually continue to draw.

Both current accounts and various types of deposit account exist. At the moment, interest on deposit accounts owned by non-residents is paid free of French withholding tax but this advantage for the UK tax resident may disappear if certain proposed EEC tax rules come into force in France.

You will be supplied with a cheque book, usually within a few weeks of opening an account. You are strongly advised to order a new cheque book at the same time as you receive your first cheque book and continuously to repeat the process. There are some special peculiarities about French bank accounts which it is essential to note.

Rules about cheques

In effect, all cheques are crossed although bearer cheques do exist. Their use, which is very rare, seems to imply to the French and their tax authorities that some kind of tax fraud is involved.

You cannot negotiate a cheque, that is, you cannot get a cheque from someone in your favour and, by signing it on the back, pass it on to a third person. Cheques can only be paid into your own account and then need endorsement as do cheques on which you draw cash for yourself at the bank.

A French cheque cannot be 'stopped' except if it has been stolen or lost and you must report this to the bank. If you stop a cheque for other reasons, the results may be curious and unexpected for the British. This involves very complicated French law and the only proper advice which can be given is that, before you do this, go to see your bank manager or your lawyer.

You cannot give a postdated cheque, that is, you *can* give it but it will be cleared on the day of its presentation whatever the date may be on the cheque.

If words and figures on a cheque do not agree, the words prevail. If a cheque is more than six months old, it will be treated as 'stale' and not cleared. Most branches of British banks would contact you in either case and query the situation, but many branches of French banks would not.

Bank drafts *(chèques de banque)* are not treated as cash as in the UK but are cleared as though they are ordinary cheques. This can be infuriating when you pay in to your branch of the X Bank an English bank draft drawn on the Paris Head Office of the X Bank only to find that you are not given immediate value for it.

Ordinary cheques take longer to clear than in the UK. Bank statements often duplicate themselves in their opening and closing entries. This, coupled with the slowness of clearing cheques means that you have to treat the balances shown on your statements with reserve. It is possible to get photocopies of paid cheques but not to get paid cheques returned with your statement. Sometimes this is necessary as the French are frequently not very good at accounting and will sometimes deny receipt of payment unless you can produce proof of the debit of the cheque. If you do not live permanently in France, make certain that statements are sent to you in the UK and not to your French address.

Special rules apply to 'bouncing' cheques but are too complicated to describe in detail here. Although it has been calculated that about one in every 1,500 cheques 'bounce', the rules are considered sufficiently effective to allow most shops to accept cheques without cheque cards merely on proof of identity. In short, if you issue a cheque which cannot be met, your bank will inform you and you have 15 days in which to put this right. If you fail to do this, your cheque book will be taken from you and you will not be allowed to issue cheques for a year or to operate any other existing account. The fact will be reported to the Banque de France which prevents you from opening any new accounts during that period and violations of this ban are reported to the police. One of the problems of this situation is that it affects an innocent joint holder of an account but equally, it can be remedied if it was caused by a genuine error.

Direct debits

This is what is known as payment by *prélèvement*. It is extremely useful in the case of electricity, gas or telephone bills since it avoids your arriving home only to find no light or telephone. The bank pays the bill but does not check it. You will be sent direct a copy of the account to check. Do not use this method for paying *taxe d'habitation* or *taxe foncière*: It is best to check these first and you are allowed plenty of time in which to pay.

How best to make use of your bank in connection with property purchases is dealt with in Chapter 4.

Property purchase loans

There are a number of French institutions in the property

mortgage market. They take the place of the UK Building
Societies although they are quite different in concept.
Virtually all the banks are also lenders for property
purchases. Each institution has its own rules but, in general,
it should be possible to borrow up to 75%, or perhaps a little
more, for a permanent home, and 50–60% for a holiday
home. The length of loans in France is shorter than in the
UK and on average 10 to 15 years would be considered
normal. An offer of a loan can usually be obtained quite
quickly. If you are buying with the aid of a loan, it is a good
idea to arrange this before signing any contract even though
there are special rules for property purchases with mortgages
(see Chapter 4).

In quite a number of cases, where the loan is less than a
certain amount or a certain percentage of value, the lender
will not have a valuation made, and when an inspection is
made of property offered for mortgage, it is generally for
valuation rather than for survey purposes. You will not,
therefore, be able to find out if there are any defects in the
property such as you can in the UK when, for example, a
building society will retain part of a loan until certain repairs
have been carried out.

Loans are available either on a building society basis with
equal repayments at stated periods, which are usually
monthly, or less frequently on a standing basis where only
interest is payable until the date of repayment of the capital
sum is due. Every lender in France requires the borrower to
effect life cover, which sometimes includes accident and
sickness cover. The premiums are not high and under 50
years of age a medical inspection is usually not required.

Protection of the borrower

There are stringent rules about mortgages for the protection
of borrowers. Reference to these is made in Chapter 4 about
the effect of these rules on purchase contracts. As between
lender and borrower, the most important are:

- every loan offer must contain full details of the terms of the loan offered and it must remain in force for 30 days
- the offer cannot be accepted before the end of a ten-day 'cooling off' period
- acceptance of an offer of a loan is subject to the condition that the loan is taken up — and therefore your purchase is completed within four months
- the loan offer may forbid early repayment of part of a loan by instalments of less than 10% of the original loan. A penalty may be charged for early repayment but it may not exceed the rate in force from time to time set by the Government
- if a borrower makes default and the lender does not call in the loan, he may instead increase the rate of interest within certain permitted limits until the borrower is no longer in default. A borrower may apply to the court for relief if, for example, he loses his job or becomes ill.

If the loan and purchase are dealt with simultaneously, there is only one document, not a separate *acte de vente* (conveyance) and mortgage, and it is preferable for a variety of practical reasons to carry out both transactions together.

8 The French tax system

Whether you are leaving the UK permanently or whether you intend to go on living here but have a holiday home in France, you must get advice from experts who know *both* French and UK tax law.

For many years the Double Tax Treaty with France has included an arrangement for the exchange between the two countries of personal tax information. At present, the link between France and the UK in tax matters is not as close as that between France and certain other countries but EEC arrangements are intended to remedy this.

The following taxes will affect you as a buyer (and on occasions as a seller), or as the owner of a house or flat, in France, irrespective of whether you live there permanently:

* stamp duties *(enregistrement)* payable on the purchase of property
* VAT *(TVA)* on the purchase of building land and on certain sales of houses and flats
* annual taxes *(taxe foncière* and *taxe d'habitation)* on the ownership and occupation of property
* capital gains tax *(plus-value)* on the sale of property
* inheritance tax *(droits de succession)*.

It is very unlikely that you will become subject to French wealth tax *(Impot de solidarité sur la Fortune)*, which is a tax on the value of capital assets payable by persons resident for tax purposes in France in respect of *all* their assets, non-residents are liable in respect of their assets in France. It is payable by private individuals only and is not payable unless your assets exceed 4,000,000 francs.

Resident or non-resident?

It is unlikely that you will be resident in France for French tax purposes unless you are also the holder of a *carte de séjour,* which confirms your right to live on a permanent basis in France. You can be resident for tax purposes in more than one country but, on the whole, this is not to be recommended. You are liable to pay French income tax (ie you are a French tax resident) if:

* you have your *foyer* or home in France. This can be where your family lives even if you spend most of your time travelling elsewhere
* your principal place of residence is France, which it is deemed to be if you spend a total of more than 183 days in any one year there
* you carry on a profession or business activity in France unless it is ancillary to a main activity carried on elsewhere
* the centre of your economic interests is in France, ie most of your investments are there or you direct your business activities (which are not in France) from France.

Do not worry that the French tax year starts on 1 January and the UK tax year on 5 April. This can cause problems if your UK income is large enough and you are liable to French tax but they can usually be sorted out if you take advice from your accountant in good time.

Domiciled or not domiciled?

This is a very important question. It affects mainly
inheritance tax, both in France and in the UK, and also what
is going to happen to everything you own when you die. The
answer can also decide if it is useful to make certain kinds of
investments. Your domicile is the place where at any moment
you intend living for the rest of your life. Often it is safer,
though sadder, to consider it as the country in which you
would prefer to die. Husbands and wives under English law
can have separate domiciles. As a general rule, the English
Revenue will fight hard to claim that you have an English
domicile if it will bring in inheritance tax. It helps them to
prove the fact if you are living abroad by giving away any
sign that England is still your home for example, in your Will
that you would like to be buried in the plot you have bought
somewhere in England.

Advertising your domicile is so important that if really you
leave England never to return but always to live in France,
you must continue to make this clear all round at every
possible opportunity.

French taxes

Enregistrement

Fortunately, the basic rate of stamp duty on the purchase of
land is virtually never exacted, for it works out at about 17%.
There is a wide variety of exceptions of which you are likely
to meet the following:

- on the purchase of all 'new' property (ie within five years
of completion of construction) from the developer himself,

and on the first sale within that period, the rate is nil but small Land Registry fees are payable on the ex-TVA price
- on other purchases of property to be used as a private dwelling house the rate is about 7%-8%
- on building land the rate is nil and no Land Registry fees are payable
- there are various reduced rates of duty applicable to land used for agricultural and other special purposes.

It is important to note that:

- when 'new' property is being sold, it is often incorrectly advertised as being sold with *'frais de notaire réduits'*. However, it is the stamp duty only which is 'reduced'; notarial fees are unaltered
- the rates quoted above are approximate. This is because stamp duties consist of departmental and local duties which vary slightly from place to place plus an overall percentage on the duty thus arrived at
- in certain cases, in order to obtain a reduced rate of stamp duty, you have to undertake to use the land or house for residential purposes within a limited period of time. Failure to do this will result in the full rate being charged plus a penalty
- where you have a house with land, an area of 2,500 or sometimes 5,000 square metres goes with the house for stamp duty purposes. The remainder of the land will be charged at a higher or possibly full rate.

French VAT (Taxe sur la valeur ajoutée – TVA)

When you buy land for building, you will pay TVA, currently at 13%. So, when a purchase price is quoted to you, you must usually add on this tax to calculate the total cost (no stamp duty is payable).

TVA will be payable on work done to build your house and the current rate is 18.6%. It is more usual in France for prices or estimates to be quoted ex-TVA *(hors taxes)* rather than TTC or *toutes taxes comprises*. (See also capital gains tax.)

When you buy 'new property', you will be quoted a price which includes TVA. The amount of this tax will be shown separately in the conveyance to you and the seller will account for it to the tax authorities. If you sell within a five-year period of completion of the property, you will be liable for TVA on the sale price and you will quote a TVA-inclusive price to your buyer. You will be liable for the TVA on the sale price less the TVA already paid on the purchase price, adjusted to take account of any changes in the rate. So, unless you sell at a considerable profit quite soon after you have bought, your TVA liability will not be large.

Annual taxes on property

These are *taxe foncière* and *taxe d'habitation*. The former is payable by the owner of property, usually quite a small amount and is calculated on notional letting values. *Taxe d'habitation* is also calculated on this basis and is payable by the occupier, whether owner or not. This tax is the equivalent of general rates in the UK and is payable to the local authority or *commune*.

Ownership and occupation are established as at 1 January in each year. Therefore, if you buy and take occupation of property on 2nd January, you will probably get a tax-free year. In theory, *taxe foncière* is apportionable between seller and buyer but this rarely happens; *taxe d'habitation* is not apportionable.

Taxe foncière is not payable during the first two years after completion of a new property. There are a number of circumstances resulting in reductions of both this and *taxe d'habitation* and it is worth while making enquiries to see if you qualify.

These and other taxes should not be paid with English cheques as this may cause problems for the local authorities. You are allowed approximately two months in which to pay and thereafter there is a 10% penalty.

Income tax

You are not liable to pay income tax simply because you have bought property in France. Indeed, you could become liable to pay French income tax without owning any property in France, although this is very unlikely. The calculation of income tax in France is as complicated as in the UK and the rates and reliefs change just as often. If you do become liable to French income tax, you can obtain help from the local tax office or from a local accountant. However, if you have any large or unusual non-French income, you should seek professional advice.

Capital gains tax

For non-residents, capital gains tax is currently at the rate of one-third of the gain on the sale of land. This is, therefore, a situation in which it is essential to have established whether or not you are resident for tax purposes in France. If you are not, you will realise the importance of the comments on CGT in Chapter 18. If you are resident, then you need not concern yourself with this tax since, as in the UK, your principal private residence is not subject to it.

Inheritance tax

Droits de succession differ radically from the English counterpart in three respects:

- it is not payable out of the estate at a rate which is linked to the value of the assets of the person who has died
- the rate at which it is paid depends on the relationship of

the beneficiary to the person who has died and each
beneficiary is liable for his own tax
• there is no surviving spouse exemption.

Wherever you are domiciled and/or resident, inheritance tax
will be payable on all your assets in France. If you are
domiciled in France, which almost certainly means that you
are also resident there for tax purposes, this tax is also
payable on all your assets outside France, wherever they may
be. The value of your estate will be calculated on one of these
bases and divided amongst your beneficiaries who will each
pay their appropriate tax. However, as in the UK, it is a tax
which is related solely to the death of a person and his assets,
and its payment does not depend on whether or not a
beneficiary who pays the tax is resident in France.

The rates of tax operate on a 'slice' basis. When the
beneficiary is a spouse, child or parent, the rate starts at 5%
on assets not exceeding 50,000 francs, progressing in stages to
20% on assets between 100,000 and 3,400,000 francs and on
again in stages to 40% for assets in excess of 11,200,000
francs. In the case of brothers and sisters, the rates are 35%
up to 150,000 francs and 45% on the balance. More distant
relations pay 55% and non-relatives pay 60%.

There are a number of reliefs of which the most important
are:

• in the case of spouses, children and parents, no tax is
payable on the first 275,000 francs
• in certain circumstances, brothers or sisters, who in any
event must have lived with the person who has died for at
least five years before their death, do not pay tax on the
first 100,000 francs
• physically or mentally handicapped beneficiaries do not
pay tax on the first 300,000 francs of what they inherit
• any beneficiary who does not benefit from any other
reduction does not pay tax on the first 10,000 francs
• beneficiaries with three or more children get a reduction
per child on the tax calculated as above.

Interest is payable on *droits de succession* from six months after the date of death of a person who dies in France and 12 months if they died outside France. Arrangements can be made for the tax to be paid by instalments or deferred in circumstances similar to those in force in the UK.

The tax on gifts *(droits de donation)* is calculated in the same manner as *droits de succession* by reference to the amount of the gift and the relationship between the maker of the gift and the receiver. However, depending on the age of the giver, there is a percentage reduction: the younger the giver, the greater is the reduction.

The impact of French inheritance tax, the manner in which it is assessed and the persons on whom it falls, coupled with French succession rules (see Chapter 15), make it essential, if you intend to acquire property in France, to take the most competent advice and to plan your investments accordingly. The terms of your Will and whether you should have a French Will and an English Will, or one only, are points of vital importance and are discussed in detail in Chapter 16.

Offshore companies

For some years, the French tax authorities have been aware that the use of non-French companies as owners of land in their country can lead to the reduction of French tax. Until a recent convention on the subject is ratified by France, trusts are unknown to French law. The successful use of a non-French company for this purpose involves a considerable amount of expert knowledge and no one should ever indulge in an exercise of this kind without it. Never take the advice of a friend who says he has avoided French tax in this way and remember that if you make a mistake it may cost a 3% tax on the *capital* value of your house or flat in France every year and the conveyance to the company will carry stamp duty at the *full* rate of approximately 20%.

9 Time-sharing

If you have had an enjoyable holiday in France, you may feel that you would like to spend many more holidays there. Of course, you can stay in a hotel but this is not the same as being in your own home. You can also rent a flat or house but it is very disappointing when, having enjoyed yourself there, you want to rent it again next year only to find that it is fully booked. Alternatively, you can buy a flat or a house but you may feel that it is expensive just to use it for two or three weeks a year.

If you have family who can use your own home in France in your absence or if you think that you would not mind letting it during the time when you cannot be there yourself, buying a flat or house may be the answer even if you can be there yourself for only a few weeks every year. But if neither of these ways of reducing the cost of owning a home in France attracts you, the answer may be time-sharing.

France is not a country which sets out to attract the foreign buyer in preference to the French buyer so that since the French are unlikely to fall for the 'get rich quick' methods of the sellers of time-shares in other countries, you will benefit from their attitude. Naturally, there are exceptions to this because you may have to buy not from the original owner of a property divided into time-shares but from someone who has owned the time-share for some time and is trying to sell it to you in England. If you follow the advice given below, you should avoid most of the problems.

The French Government has tried to protect people from the misleading technical terms used to describe time-sharing. By the use of the word *propriété* (ownership) linked to other words which have no meaning in French law, sellers of time-shares implied that the buyer was getting full ownership of a flat. In addition, although the concept of time-sharing is simple enough, it was not covered by the legal system.

The costs of time-sharing

As the word implies, time-sharing means that instead of buying a flat outright, you buy the right to occupy it for a specified period in each year. In France, time-sharing is almost exclusively limited to flats but it can also apply to houses.

The period in the year during which you can occupy the flat and the number of occasions in a year when you can exercise that right set the price you pay. For example, if the flat is in an area where the holiday season is in summer, July and August will cost more than January or February. If it is in a ski resort, the winter months will be more expensive than the summer months.

In some cases, you may be able to exchange your time-share period for a period in another flat either in France or elsewhere. You will almost always be able to allow someone else to occupy the flat during your time-share period and it will be very rare to find any restrictions on selling it.

In addition to paying the price of your time-share, you will be required to contribute to the overall cost of managing the block which contains the flat you occupy. The method of calculating this is explained later in this chapter.

This chapter assumes that your time-sharing block was built or adapted so that the original seller of the time-sharing periods was a single person, or a company owning the whole block. The management of the block, the amount of control you have over the quality of the management, and its cost to you, depend on which method is used to set up the time-sharing scheme. Sometimes, you will find that one person owns two or three flats, not the whole block, and then sets up a time-sharing scheme just for those flats. This may cause problems and it is best to avoid buying a time-share in these circumstances.

Some general guidelines

The Office of Fair Trading in London has issued guidelines for those buying a time-share outside the UK. Because of recent changes in the French law on time-sharing, these now contain good advice in connection with the purchase of almost any kind of property and do not apply specifically to French time-shares. Remember:

- never to sign any contract or document under pressure or without having it explained to you by a lawyer who knows both French and English law. It is very unlikely that your solicitor in England himself will be able to advise you unless he has had a number of years' practical experience in France
- to ask carefully about maintenance costs and expect that they will be underestimated. Some amenities may not be originally provided but will subsequently become necessary and their cost will probably fall not on the seller but on the time-sharers
- to make certain that you have someone in France who can look after your interests
- to make sure you know exactly what it is you are buying, that you can afford it and, above all, never think of buying a time-share as an investment.

Old system *v* new system

There are now two different legal systems in France for time-sharing. Under the old system, you bought the right to occupy a flat for a given period of time between given dates. This right was not 'land' as a lease is 'land' so that it could not be registered anywhere. It was merely a contract between you and (usually) the owner of the block allowing you on a personal basis to occupy the flat in exchange for which you paid a lump sum and then an annual sum to cover your maintenance charges. The original owner (or possibly someone else he designated) was responsible for maintaining the block, cleaning your flat before you arrived and after you left. From a practical point of view, if the flat was badly managed, there was little you could do and, in general, the time-sharer was at the mercy of the maintenance set-up against which there was no simple method of enforcing complaints. As to the amount of service charges, these were extremely difficult to check and almost impossible to control.

The new system which came into force in 1986 makes use of a type of French company which owns the whole block housing the time-share flats. You buy not a time-share but shares in the company, which give you the right to occupy a particular flat during a designated period. The main points to note are that:

- this modern method is not obligatory. However, prospective time-sharers are well-advised to try to find a block where it is being used. For some time to come, this may mean that it will be desirable to buy time-shares in a new building rather than from an existing time-share owner
- the type of company used (a *société civile d'attribution*) is really no more than a partnership but when this is used for a time-sharing scheme it gives the shareholders the same protection as though they were shareholders in a UK limited company
- all decisions relating to all aspects of the time-sharing

scheme are taken by the shareholders at company meetings. In this way, the time-sharers are masters of their own destiny provided they are sensible enough to exercise their rights.

Most company decisions are by simple majority and shareholders (ie the time-sharers) may and should appoint proxies unless they are certain of being able to attend meetings and are fairly fluent in French.

The shareholders appoint (and can dismiss) a managing agent who manages the block, pays bills, negotiates contracts, employs staff etc and, of course, is accountable to the shareholders. The annual service charge is fixed on the basis of these accounts after approval by the time-sharers at a company meeting.

The way in which a time-share block is managed under this new system is much the same as for a condominium (see Chapter 10). In both cases, your presence at meetings personally or by a proxy is necessary. It is inevitable in the case of a time-share company that a considerable number of shareholders must be absent from their flats when meetings are held and you may find it useful to make use of MPOA to vote on your behalf (see Chapter 10). Company meetings are not usually held in English even if the majority of shareholders are British and all correspondence will be in French.

Ownership of a time-share period through the ownership of shares is safer than under the old system. The new system allows time-sharers to take part in their own management and the ownership of the shares which allow you to occupy your time-share flat is a matter of record. Under the old system, the contract was a private one between you and the owner of the block only and was of no value as between one time-sharer and another or indeed anyone else. Your right to occupy a flat under the old system and your shares in the time-sharing company under the newer system can pass under your Will in English law.

There are special rules about the documents to be used when buying (or afterwards transferring) shares in a time-sharing company: they tell you everything you need to know about the company and about your rights. If you are buying under the old system, there is no obligation to provide any kind of information but it is essential that you demand as much as you can. In any case, whether under the old or the new system do not try to be your own lawyer: use your local legal expert and through him, under the new scheme, the services of a *notaire*.

If you buy under the old system, all you will receive is a contract which sets out rights and liabilities and the transaction cannot be registered anywhere.

If you buy under the new system, you will receive a copy of the Articles of Association *(Statuts)* of the company of which you are a shareholder. These will set out the rules for the management of the company and the time-sharing scheme and will show the flat and the period(s) of occupation allotted to you by the shares you have bought. It is not customary for French companies of this kind to issue share certificates. You can prove your ownership of your shares by the confirmation of the managing agent and every transfer of shares must be notified to, and approved by, the company.

In France, a fairly new and rather unusual form of time-sharing *(bi-propriété)* exists which divides the year into two parts and only two owners are involved. This produces an interest in land which can be registered at the French Land Registry. It is a mixture of ordinary joint ownership and time-sharing and, if it is offered to you, it is important to seek advice.

10 Life in a condominium

Since French law requires that any building, parts of which are owned by different people, must be treated as a *copropriété*, or condominium, it is certain that if you buy a flat in France you will buy it *en copropriété*. There will also be occasions when you buy a house, or land on which you build a house, on a building estate *(lotissement)* where the *copropriété* will play an important part in your life. Although your house will be your own individual property, the parts of the estate which are used by all the house owners, such as the access roads, possibly the gardens of each house and all the amenities on the estate — the swimming-pool and the tennis-courts — will be owned jointly by the house owners.

Costs of flat ownership

The French have more experience than the British of living in flats and of sharing the cost of maintaining a block. Various methods of sharing costs have been tried; the current method, which dates from 1965, is to divide the cost of managing a block roughly according to the value of each flat based on a number of factors. However, as this calculation is often made before the block is built, there is little point in using your percentage share of the service charges as a guide to the current value of your flat.

The system of *copropriété* is unknown in England and it would be a great pity if it were allowed to take over from the existing English system of buying a flat by taking a long lease from the owner of the block or by taking over the lease from an existing flat owner. However, one advantage of the French system is that the rules and regulations which govern the management of a French condominium must abide by the Law passed in 1965 (as from time to time amended) so that neither developers nor the flat owners themselves can make rules which are unreasonably restrictive or unfair.

Systems of flat ownership

There are several basic differences between the French and the English systems. In England, the usual system is for each flat owner to own his own flat but not to have interest in the common parts of the block: the roof, the staircases, the drains etc. In France, you own your flat but, in addition, you have a share in all the common parts of the block, including the surrounding land, swimming-pool etc.

Under an English long lease of a flat, you have many obligations to your landlord; your landlord probably has many less towards you but they will include maintaining the block in exchange for which you pay a service charge. In France, you have no landlord. You have a similar list of obligations and the liability to pay a service charge which are contained in a document called *règlement de copropriété* but your obligations are towards your co-flat owners. In England, therefore, you have a number of flat owners on the one hand, often represented by a Tenants' Association, and a landlord (or possibly a management company) on the other. In France, every flat owner has obligations towards every other flat owner.

In France, everything to do with a condominium, its rules, its management and the part you are expected to play in it, is in French, this is part of 'living abroad'.

Finally, you must get used to the fact that the ownership of a flat in France is neither freehold nor leasehold. This need not cause you any problems and you are free to sell it, let it, mortgage it, give it away or leave it by Will. The easiest way to treat it is as a freehold which has no land attached to it.

Obligations and liabilities

Before you complete the purchase of a flat, you should get a copy of the *règlement de copropriété*, which sets out your obligations and liabilities as a flat owner. You should ask for a copy of this from an existing owner before you sign a contract to buy and from the developer of a new block before you sign any contract with him. Although it is desirable to see this document as early as possible, as most of them are drawn up by notaries and either incorporate or refer to the Law of 1965 (with some recent amendments), it is not a disaster if you cannot. If, however, you are buying a flat in a building built before 1965, you should make more persistent enquiries.

This is because either you will have a *règlement de copropriété* which was drawn up before that date and so must be read as amended by current Laws or because there is no such document and the co-owners must rely entirely on those Laws for information. There is just a possibility that if there has been no sale of a flat for a very long time, the method of ownership of the flat is not direct but through the ownership of shares in a company which gives the right to the occupation of the flat (see Chapter 9 on time-sharing for a modern use of this method). This method of owning flats is now seldom come across and all that need be said is that if it should apply to a flat you are buying, you will need special explanations from your adviser.

When you manage to obtain a *règlement de copropriété*, which is often combined with a *cahier des charges* and sometimes loosely called by either name, you will find that it contains the division of the block into *lots,* giving each lot its share or *quote-part* in the communal areas of the block. *Quote-parts* are usually expressed as fractions of 1,000 or 10,000. The document will also contain:

- the share of service charges attributed to each *lot*
- rules about the calculation and payment of service charges
- a list of what each flat owner may and may not do
- rules applying to the management of the block
- rules applying to meetings of flat owners
- a variety of rules dealing with certain eventualities, such as if the block is burnt down, if additions to the block are made or if it is desired to join two flats together, etc.

Service charges

These may be divided into general and special charges. General charges will apply to expenses common to all flats; special charges are those applicable to individual blocks in a complex or, more unusually, to a flat or group of flats which enjoy an amenity which the others do not. Usually, general charges will be the same proportion of the total general management expenses as your *quote-part* and, in most cases, the proportion of service charges payable by a flat is unalterable.

Service charges are based on an annual budget presented to the Annual General Meeting of the flat owners. It is customary to collect these charges in advance by two, three or four instalments each year, depending on how much cash in hand is needed at any one time, and the final instalment in every year is a 'topping up' payment. Sometimes an additional payment is asked for either to cover a special item of expenditure or to ensure that there is always something in the management 'kitty' or *fonds de roulement.* Failure to pay service charges will result in the payment of interest and ultimately legal action. Service charge accounts are not always easy to follow but the *syndic*, or managing agent, should be able to explain them to you.

What you may and what you may not do

In general, you may make alterations to the inside of your flat provided that you do not interfere with any of the common parts of the building. You would be wise to discuss any major alteration with the *syndic* (see below) in case what you have in mind requires consent. You must be careful with balconies and terraces which might seem to be part of your flat but which are in fact a common part of the building. This prevents you, for example, from repainting your terrace yourself.

You will certainly be required to conform to the standard type and pattern of exterior blinds and urged not to dry clothes on your balconies. Domestic animals are normally permitted but parking your car, except in designated parking spaces, is forbidden.

You will be required to insure your own flat in respect of certain risks and usually to produce a certificate of insurance to the *syndic* (see Chapter 12 for insurance of property). Overall insurance of the block is the responsibility of the condominium as a whole and forms part of your service charge.

You must use your flat only in accordance with the purposes permitted in the *règlement de copropriété* and this will normally be as a private dwelling house. However, mixed, private and professional users are common in France and, if you want to practise as a doctor, dentist or architect etc from a flat, you will probably be allowed to do so.

Management of the block

The flat owners as a group form a *syndicat* and appoint a

Points to note

1 You will be amazed at what a French landlord asks for in the way of references. Apart from rent receipts for many years past, which you will not be able to give if you own your house in England, he may ask for income tax receipts and bank statements. If you use a branch of a 'British' bank in France, ask the manager to phone the landlord's agents and to speak in your favour. It is unlikely that you will ever miss a lease because you cannot provide what is asked for and you can usually come to some sort of compromise.

2 A lease must be in writing. It is illegal for the tenant to be asked to pay more than one-half of the landlord's agents' commission.

3 The fixing of the rent which may be charged is quite complex and may ultimately be a matter for the court. You must make careful enquiries to be sure you are not overcharged. If the lease contains a rent revision clause it can only take effect once each year and the revision must be linked to the Cost of Construction Index.

4 It is highly desirable, but not obligatory, to have prepared an *état des lieux* (schedule of condition) when you move into the premises. Make sure that this is prepared meticulously. Your landlord will insist on another *état des lieux* (schedule of dilapidations) being taken on your departure and this is why it is so necessary to have the two schedules available for comparison.

5 If you do not pay rent in advance at intervals of more than two months, you may be required to pay a deposit, which may not exceed two months' rent which may not be used for unpaid rent during the term of the lease. When you leave, the deposit must be returned to you within two months of your quitting the premises less any amount you may owe the landlord for dilapidations.

6   You will pay in addition a small annual stamp duty on
    leases.

Repairs

It is inevitable that the flat you rent will be in a
condominium. The repairs of all the common parts of the
building, for which you as a tenant are not liable, are the
liability of the condominium as a whole. That same liability
will, as between you and the landlord, be his liability and his
alone. This is the cause of many problems. For example, if
your flat is on the top floor and the roof starts to leak, only
the *syndic* of the condominium can repair it but he has no
duty towards you to do so. As far as you are concerned, it is
your landlord who is liable to get the roof repaired but he is
not allowed to do it himself. If you complain to your
landlord, he will ask you to complain to the *syndic*. There is
no way of avoiding this but it stresses the need to rent a flat
only in a block which is in a good state of repair.

Insurance

Because of the landlord's liability for repairs, make sure that
you are fully insured for contents and other internal risks.
Your lease will require you to insure against 'tenant's risks',
which is a type of comprehensive cover for the interior of the
flat and for damage which the flat might do to others, for
example, if the bath water overflows. You are free to choose
your insurance company; the landlord cannot compel you to
use a particular company.

Service charges

The law states which items in the service charges a landlord
may pass on to a tenant. Normally, you will be asked to make
payments on account with your rent and, once a year, you
will be supplied with extracts from the landlord's service
charges accounts, when you will be asked to pay the balance.
You cannot attend meetings of the flat owners but you can
insist upon evidence from your landlord in support of his
demands.

Since it is so easy to extricate yourself from a lease, leases
cannot be assigned without your landlord's consent, which he
is not obliged to give. Subletting is permitted with the
consent of the landlord, who is entitled to know what rent
you are charging the subtenant.

Tenants are protected in possession. Private individuals must
grant three year leases and company landlords leases lasting
six years. If the landlord does not give notice to quit at the
end of the lease, it is automatically renewed for the same
period. A landlord may, however, offer a new lease on other
terms provided they comply with the law.

If a landlord has special professional or personal reasons
which are stated in the lease to retake possession within the
three year period (but not in the first year), he may do so.
However, he must give two months notice and if the event he
is relying on does not happen, he cannot rely on it later. In
order to obtain possession at the end of a lease, the landlord
must either prove he has 'legitimate and serious' reasons for
so doing or that he wishes to live in the premises himself. He
may also give notice if he wishes to sell, the tenant then has a
two month option to buy at the open market price, if he
refuses and the landlord sells to another at a lower price, the
tenant may (if he ever finds out) require the sale to him at
that price. There are special rules for the protection of elderly
tenants.

12 Settling in

Assume that you have bought your property and have chosen
it to suit your future intentions. It may be just a holiday
home or it may be that you have decided to live in France on
a permanent basis. Or it may be that it is a holiday home
which will become your permanent home on retirement. As
discussed in Chapter 8, it is very unlikely that you will
become liable to French income tax unless you have your
permanent home in France. However, if you obtain the
necessary permission to reside permanently in France, you
will become liable and will have to make the appropriate
arrangements.

Applying for permanent residence

Visa de longue durée

Because you are a citizen of an EC country you automatically
have certain rights to reside and to work in every other EC
country. In practice, this freedom is limited to some extent
because most countries like to keep a check on the entry of
foreigners even if they come from another EC country. You
need formal permission to reside in France on a permanent
basis. However, as a British citizen, you may stay in the
country for three months at a time without any formalities.

If you intend to take up residence permanently in France, you must apply to one of the French Consulates in the UK for a *visa de longue durée*. This involves completing a form and providing evidence that:

* you have somewhere to live in France
* you have an income sufficient to keep you from being a burden on the French State
* you have a medical certificate.

Proof of a home in France can either be a copy of the lease or conveyance to you of your home, or you can ask the notary who dealt with the purchase to give you an *attestation d'acquisition* to prove the purchase. On the whole, the *attestation* is more useful as you will probably need it again for the import of your furniture; it is one sheet in length and photocopies are accepted. The average *acte de vente* may be at least 20-pages long and is often not available until several months after you have completed your purchase.

Carte de séjour

It takes about six weeks to obtain a *visa de longue durée*. You need to take this (it is stamped in your passport) to your local *bureau des étrangers* in France and, in exchange, you will be given a receipt entitling you to a *carte de séjour* which is initially valid for one year.

This is the procedure which any French Consulate in England will advise you to follow. In fact, it may be possible to short-circuit the procedure depending on where you are intending to live. The *préfet* of each *département* in France is authorised to grant *cartes de séjour* directly to EEC citizens without the production of a *visa de longue durée*. There is no list showing which *préfet* will exercise his discretion to do this and so you must make enquiries in the area where you will be living.

Your 'papers'

Generally, the French have a very relaxed attitude towards
'papers'. French identity cards are not obligatory (although a
Frenchman without one would be highly suspect) and you
are not required to carry any other form of identification.
However, to avoid complications with the CRS (or riot
police) it is useful to have your *carte de séjour* available and
this also serves as identification when you make payments by
cheque.

When any kind of identity document is needed, you must
obtain at least three passport-size photographs of yourself.
Remember that *timbres fiscaux*, with which you pay for the
document you want, are obtainable at some tobacconists but
never at a post office.

Your car

As soon as you have a *carte de séjour* you must apply for a
French driving licence and if your car has British plates you
must re-register it. Normally, you will be given back your
UK licence once all the details have been taken from it but
the French do check with Swansea.

Making the move

Few people are likely to buy furnished property in France
and it is advisable not to do so. You must, therefore, decide
whether to export your own furniture from the UK or to buy
afresh in France. If you are making a permanent move, you
will probably prefer to take your own things with you. In
many cases, this will be a sensible decision because many

items are more expensive in France and some, such as carpets, curtains and silverwear are, in general, of a lower quality. However, if you are going to live in one of the hotter parts of France your furniture will probably be unsuitable: on the Mediterranean coast, where you can live out of doors for six months of the year, the hot sunshine and the salt atmosphere of the sea ruins antique or good-quality furniture.

Importing furniture can be relatively relaxed providing the correct procedure is followed. Hiccups can occur, however, as a result of the inconsistency of operating this procedure through different regions of France. The interpretation at the port can be somewhat different to that of a local office in the south, for example, and the paperwork can be horrendous.

It is worth remembering also that you will not be allowed to sell any imported furniture in France for ten years.

Importing duty-free goods

The rules governing the import of duty and tax-free household goods to furnish a home in France are simple and generous. Provided that you have owned the goods for at least three months and have paid VAT on them in the UK (antiques are free in any case) you may freely import all your personal belongings, furniture and furnishings, either in one consignment or over a period of 12 months, for use in your new permanent home. All that is needed is an inventory (in French) in duplicate and a copy of a lease or the *attestation d'acquisition* to prove you have a home in France. The procedure is slightly different for the furnishing of a holiday home, when you are limited to items reasonably needed for this type of a home. In this case, you must send an inventory (in French) in triplicate to the Regional Director of Customs in the area where your holiday home is and, in due course, you will receive back the necessary authority.

A basic knowledge of French should suffice for the inventory: there is absolutely no need to spend money on using a translation service. Remember that your television will be useless in France if it is not dual standard because the French use the SECAM system. Otherwise, all electrical equipment used in the UK can be used in France although you should check microwave ovens some of which are electrically suitable only for the country in which they are sold.

These rules are based on procedures used in all EEC countries so they should not vary. It is, however, as well to check them at the time you want to make use of them. It is not safe to rely either on French Consulates or removal firms; the safest thing to do if you are not in France yourself is to ask a friend in France to obtain the latest Customs leaflet.

Using a removal firm

Although the French Customs procedures are very simple, it is worth while using a firm with international experience to move your goods to France. You may be surprised at how expensive such a move can be and it is advisable to get several estimates. If you do not have too much furniture, try to arrange a part load so that you are sharing the cost with someone else.

In theory, it is possible to do the removal job yourself. In practice, French Customs will deal only with a *transitaire* or customs agent who will, for a fee, arrange the formalities on your behalf.

Insurance

It is standard procedure for most removal firms not to accept liability for loss or damage to your goods in transit. It is advisable to arrange insurance yourself against every possible misfortune that could overtake your goods. There is no problem about values, which should be realistic for insurance purposes, since whatever these may be, duties are not normally payable in France. If you are tempted to do your own removal, you may find that insurance companies are unwilling to insure your belongings.

13 Factors to bear in mind

Whatever you may buy in France — flat or house, new or old — there are a number of points which need special thought.

Utilities

Water

There is absolutely no problem with water in France: it is safe to drink, although the French often prefer to drink bottled water. In general, the water is hard in France with the possible exception of Brittany, Normandy, parts of south-west France and around Grenoble.

It is not the quality of the water which is a problem but that, in certain parts of France which are liable to drought, you may find if you are living in the country that the supply is turned off occasionally. This happens in the UK as well but sufficiently rarely for you not to consider installing a storage tank as a matter of course. It pays in France to make enquiries about this and have a tank of about 1,000 litres for household purposes and, if you are a keen gardener and are allowed to do so, another tank of some 20,000 litres. If your supply is not mains, it is worth while testing it for purity from time to time or installing a filter, but the occasions when this would be necessary will be extremely rare.

What is much more important if you are buying a country property is to make absolutely sure before you buy that you have an undoubted source of water which belongs to you and cannot be turned off by your neighbour or drained away by surrounding owners. Much country property depends on local wells for water and it is often difficult to establish from the title deeds who owns them and who has the right to share them.

Virtually all water not from private supplies comes from the local *compagnie des eaux* which is sometimes owned by the local authority and sometimes is privately owned. Such water is metered and usually paid for half-yearly. When you build a new house yourself, you must get the meter installed by the local water company which charges you for this work.

Electricity

The voltage in France is 220 with the usual tolerance. Wiring is supposed to be in accordance with EC rules but frequently is not, although the green/yellow earth wire is fairly universal. Electricité de France (EDF) is the sole supplier and normally will provide a supply even in the depths of the country although this could be expensive if you are the only consumer in the area. When you install electricity for the first time in a new property which you yourself have built or had built for you, you must produce a *certificat de conformité* to prove that the wiring is up to standard. On a change of ownership, EDF may check the wiring if it is an old house but frequently they do not.

Bills are rendered every two months, alternatively estimated and actual. Payment of their accounts can be done in various ways. If you do not want to pay by direct debit, you can arrange to pay monthly but, unless you are living permanently in France, direct debit is the only method of payment which will ensure that you do not arrive at your French home only to find neither light nor heating.

Electricity or gas bill

```
        BP79 06002 NICE CEDEX        Référ 25410 208 139 291 120      01/06/89 ②
        23 N.DAME 8 GARIBALDI                                        
Tél. renseignements   93559300          ①                           4E 407
Tél. dépannage électricité 93550660                                 
Tél. dépannage gaz    93 26 22 33                                   89097
                                        Nom et adresse du distributeur de la facture
   MONTANT A REGLER      AVANT LE                                   4101252
      ③  893,59F ④ 15/06/89

   Nous vous remercions de bien vouloir régler cette facture
   par l'un des moyens proposés au verso (partie inférieure)
   .........................................
```

CONSOMMATIONS	⑤	Comp teur n°	Relevé des compteurs			Coef. ficient	Consomma tion en kWh
			nouveau	ancien	différence		
ELECTRICITE TARIF 024 HC HEURES CREUSES		524	02298	01810	488		488
HP HEURES PLEINES			03195	02512	683		683

```
HEURES CREUSES ELEC.  23H00-7H00                    Prochaine facture vers le 03/10/89
```

DÉTAIL DE LA FACTURATION HORS TAXES ⑥	Consomma tion en kWh	Prix unitaire en francs	Montant hors taxes en francs	Total HT par tarif en francs
ELECTRICITE TARIF 024 PUISSANCE 6 KW				
– ABONNEMENT				
. 57,32F/MOIS DU 25/05/89 AU 25/09/89			22928	22928
– CONSOMMATION HC DU 25/01/89 AU 25/05/89	488	* 02905	14176	
.110 JOURS A 0,2903F + 10 JOURS A 0,2932F				
SOIT 120 JOURS A 0,2905 F				
– CONSOMMATION HP DU 25/01/89 AU 25/05/89	683	* 05116	34942	49118
.110 JOURS A 0,5112F + 10 JOURS A 0,5163F				
SOIT 120 JOURS A 0,5116 F				

```
AU10/10/88,SUR LE SEUL MONTANT DE L'ABONNEMENT DES TARIFS DOMESTIQUES,LE TAUX
DE LA TVA EST PASSE DE 18,6 A 5,5 .VOTRE FACTURE TIENT COMPTE DE CETTE BAISSE   .
```

```
  *   POUR MIEUX VOUS SERVIR,NOUS REORGANISONS L'ACTIVITE RELEVE.        *
  * CE CHANGEMENT VA MODIFIER VOTRE VOS  REFERENCE S  D'ABONNEMENT S ,   *
  *      ET POURRA DECALER DE QUELQUES JOURS NOTRE FACTURATION.          *
  *          MERCI PAR AVANCE DE VOTRE COMPREHENSION                     *
  * PRIX MOYEN SUITE AU CHANGEMENT DE PRIX DE L'ELECTRICITE DU 15/05/89
```

CALCUL DES TAXES ET RECAPITULATION	TVA	Montant HT par tarif	TVA %	Taxes locales 80-40%	Montant TTC en Francs
ELECTRICITE TARIF 024 ABONNEMENT	5,50	22928	1261	2201	26390
⑦ CONSOMMATION	18,60	49118	9136	4715	62969

TOTAL FACTURE		72046	10397	6916	89359
MONTANT A REGLER				⑧	89359

Key

1 Address and phone numbers of electricity/gas company
2 Date of bill
3 Total amount of bill
4 Last date for payment
5 Meter readings and consumption in kwh
6 Details of electricity/gas consumed
7 Calculation of TVA and local tax
8 Total amount of bill

Gas

Except in towns, you must expect not to have mains gas. Where you do, you will find the system very much as for electricity: you will only be given a supply if your own piping is in order and you will be charged in the same way as for electricity.

Where you do not have a supply of town gas (and this includes not only villages and deep country but also houses and flats in towns where the builders have not provided gas) you must rely on bottled gas and this is a common practice. This will affect your insurance premium. In the case of country properties, if you are using gas only to cook, a bottle of gas will suffice and will last an average family for about six weeks. Remember always to have a spare bottle. If your hot water system and/or central heating system is also by gas, you will need a gas tank. These tanks are subject to very strict safety regulations and can be sited only in certain places on a property. This is best left to the suppliers of your gas to deal with. In many cases, you will get a free installation in exchange for using a chosen supplier's gas.

Telephone

The French have a fairly efficient telephone system although the lack of an operator can be frustrating as there is no one available to provide general help. However, there is Minitel, a small computer which will provide you with phone numbers and a vast amount of information and which is supplied free or at very little cost by France Télécom. However, to make full use of this service you must have an up-to-date 'Listel' which is not provided by France Télécom but can be bought from bookshops and stalls.

There is usually little delay in obtaining a phone except perhaps in very remote areas when this has to be done by a visit to your local *Agence Commerciale*. As soon as a line is available, you will get a letter confirming the number you have been given and that you have a *ligne mixte*. This is not a shared line but a line which will take both incoming and outgoing calls. If there is a waiting list for phones and you need one urgently — if you are an invalid, for example — a doctor's letter or similar support will give you priority.

Phone bills come every two months and can be paid by direct debit from your bank or by cash at a post office or *Agence Commerciale* or by cheque to a local area office. If you think it unlikely that you will be overcharged, it is best to pay by *prélèvement* or by direct debit. If you want a receipt for the payment, you must pay with cash.

Be careful about the use of phones you have bought yourself. France Télécom offers quite a wide variety but if you care for none of these, try to buy a phone which is *agrée* or approved. Other varieties can land you in trouble as can cordless phones which are 'tolerated'. On the whole, phones, fax machines, etc not bought in France may be difficult to get repaired.

Telephone bill

1   Date of account
2   Dates of two-month rental period (payable in advance)
3   Cost of unit (which varies according to place called and time of call)
4   Number of units recorded during period covered by account
5   Period covered by account
6   Number of account (there are six per year)
7   Details of special items to be debited or credited
8   Address and phone number of local Manager's office
9   Amount of two months' rent payable
10   Total cost of calls automatically registered
11   Special services
12   Special reductions in cost of special services
13   Total of account and last date for payment

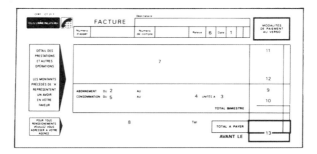

A detailed list of all calls is available for a small additional
monthly charge if the subscriber is on an 'electronic'
exchange

1 Number called of which for secrecy reasons the last four
   figures are not shown
2 Indication of foreign country or *département* or telephone
   area called
3 Indication of application of a reduced rate
4 Subscriber's phone number
5 Number of telephone account
6 Cost of call
7 Total cost of calls not shown on detailed list
8 Total amount of all calls carried to main account

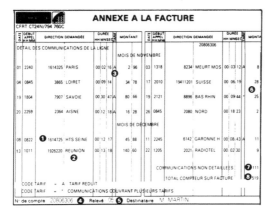

Television

France uses a different system from the UK so unless you have a dual-standard set, it is pointless taking your set to France.

Sewage

If you are in the country, it is very probable that your house or block of flats will be connected not to main drainage but to a septic tank. Rules about these differ very much from those in the UK and their construction is strictly regulated. If you have your own private septic tank, make certain that you know how often it needs emptying and where you go to have this done. If you are building your own house, make certain that the septic tank is placed where it can be reached easily and that you know exactly where it is.

Running costs and maintenance

When considering the cost of property in France do not forget that once you have paid for the property, you will be involved in annual running costs. These may include:

- standing charges for electricity, gas, telephone, etc which have to be paid whether or not you are using the property
- local taxes if you are only a tenant but both these and property tax if you are an owner and occupier
- service charges, if you live in a condominium (see Chapter 10)
- insurance premiums on both your property and its contents.

At the time you think of buying, it should be possible to assess the total of all these liabilities but to predict what they will be in a few years' time is far more difficult. Remember that a seller of property, and even more so his agent, is liable to quote figures for outgoings at the lower end of the scale and, if you cannot get independent advice on this, add on 20% to the figures you are given for safety.

If you live in a flat, the cost of maintaining your block and its surrounds will be included in your service charge, but you will also want to maintain the interior. If you live in a house, both exterior and interior are your direct concern. Property prices vary widely within France and, where property is expensive, workmen tend to be expensive so that you must also expect considerable price variations when it comes to maintenance.

Insurance

This is a particularly difficult problem. What you are looking for with any insurance company is one which:

- speaks your language so that you can understand its policies. This will not be found in France unless you happen to buy in an area where there are a lot of British owners and even then there will be problems about explaining to you the differences between English and French policies
- will deal kindly but fairly with you when you have a claim and on the whole assume that you are not making false claims
- is one from which you can easily separate yourself if you think it has not behaved properly. This cannot be done in the same way as in the UK because you cannot, except in special circumstances such as on a sale of a property, cancel policies at will. Merely not to pay a renewal premium does not result in the policy lapsing; it carries on and you remain liable for the premium unless you have given the necessary amount of notice to the insurance

company that you do not wish to renew. This notice is frequently as long as three months.

At present, (with one exception) whether you insure your property and its contents through a French or a British company, you will get a French policy. There are British companies which will readily insure French properties and their contents but they do this through their French offices or agencies. Even if you have dealt only with the company in the UK and therefore think you are getting an English policy, you will get a French policy.

In addition, where contents and jewellery are concerned, there are valuation difficulties if any of the items have been bought in the UK, as French and English values differ considerably. The answer to this is to take out insurance with Lloyd's, either in England through a Lloyd's broker or in France through a Lloyd's recognised agent, and they will issue English policies subject to English law.

Whoever you insure with will take into account any period during which your home is left unoccupied and, generally, if you are absent for more than three months in any one year, your premium will be considerably increased. You may also find that during the time you are away, you will not get certain covers, although some companies will maintain these covers if you pay more premium. In certain parts of France, such as the Côte d'Azur, premiums are higher because there are increased risks of burglary not by professional thieves but by amateurs or even tourists.

If you do have to make a claim as the result of any criminal activity it is necessary to support any claim by a *certificat de perte* from the police showing that you have reported the matter to them. Not to report a break-in to the police is considered evidence that it never occurred. If you have to make a claim for any non-criminal damage of any importance, it is worth while considering whether to ask a *hussier* (similar to a bailiff) to make a *constat* or report. Such *constats* are treated as gospel so that the insurance company cannot deny what has happened.

14 Health and health insurance

Holiday insurance for tourists

It is a false economy not to take out health insurance when you go abroad. A large number of British insurance companies offer policies to cover everything you might need if you fall ill or have an accident when you are on holiday. Your travel agent will organise a policy for you or, if you are making your own travel arrangements, ask your insurance broker to do it for you. Make certain that the policy covers you for repatriation to the UK if this becomes necessary. If you already have a private health policy, you may find that it will cover you on holiday but you must make enquiries about the extent of this cover. You will probably find that it is available only for a number of weeks per year and there may be special rules if you travel out of western Europe; check also the repatriation situation.

You should insure your baggage when you travel as a protection against airlines losing your baggage or against thieves breaking into your car.

Reciprocal medical care

You can rely on the EC reciprocal medical care arrangements alone when you go to France, by obtaining a

Form E111 before you leave the UK. However, you would not be sensible to rely on this only. The system works well provided you are happy to be treated in a *hopital conventioné*, which is similar to a National Health hospital in the UK. Often such a hospital will admit you and treat you without cost on the basis of a Form 111 alone but sometimes you are asked to pay in advance leaving you to recover your payment once you have returned to Britain. In some cases, it is necessary to contact the DSS Overseas Branch in Newcastle to ask for a Form 112 to be sent to you, which is what the French call a *prise en charge*. This form allows you to have treatment without payment.

You can also get treatment from doctors but you will almost certainly have to pay a fee. You can usually claim this back later but the proportion you receive will depend on whether you have consulted a doctor wholly within the French NHS or one who is in the scheme but who is permitted to charge higher fees. Before you leave home, it is also worth while making enquiries about the International Association for Medical Assistance to Travellers (IAMAT), which provides English-speaking doctors in many of the large towns in France who charge reduced fees. Its European office is at 57, Voirets, Grand Lancy, Geneva, Switzerland. Local Consuls will also provide the names of suitable doctors and hospitals.

You will have no difficulty in finding chemists in France. At least in the larger towns, you should be able to get the medicines you are used to at home although they may be sold under another name. It is sensible, however, to take your own supply of drugs from the UK if you are on a special course of treatment. Chemists in France are closed on Monday morning but there is always one 'duty' chemist (*pharmacie de garde*) in every town open then and also in the evenings and at weekends.

Medical provision for residents

The French National Health Scheme (*Sécurité Sociale*) is available to UK nationals who become resident in France in three circumstances:

- if you are working in France, you will be obliged, just as anyone working in the UK is obliged, to join the French NHS. The contribution you will pay will depend on your income. However, since the French scheme does not normally pay 100% of your medical bills, you will be advised and probably compelled to join a *mutuelle* (there is one for virtually every type of job in France) which will pay the balance of the cost of medicines and treatment
- if you are living in France but not working, you may join the NHS and a *mutuelle* if you wish. Your contribution will be based on your income which means that you have to submit a copy of your last tax return or be assessed at the highest rate which is over 60,000 francs a year. In this case, you would normally be well-advised to take out private medical insurance in the UK (see below) and rely on it alone
- if you are living in France and have reached retirement age, you will be in receipt of a UK retirement pension and so you (and your spouse) will be entitled to the medical benefits of the French NHS free of all contributions. All you need to do is to obtain from the DSS in Newcastle a Form E121 and present this to the *Relations Internationales* department of *Sécurité Sociale* in your area and you will be registered and issued with a card and a number. Of course, if you go to France before you reach retirement age and keep up your DSS contributions or have sufficient contributions to give you a retirement pension, you will be sent automatically a Form E121 at the right time. If you were in the French scheme before, and paying contributions, these will now cease.

Sécurité Sociale

Very briefly, the French system works as follows. All visits to the doctor, items bought from a chemist and treatments such as X-rays, blood tests etc are recorded on a brown-and-white sheet of paper called a *feuille de soins*. In the case of treatment, it is signed by the doctor or other person giving the treatment. In the case of medicines, the chemist detaches a label (*vignette*) from the container and attaches it to your *feuille de soins*. In the case of a doctor, you pay him and send off your *feuille de soins* (having kept a photocopy) to your local *Sécurité Sociale* and you will receive reimbursement of the appropriate amount. This varies according to the treatment and the status of the doctor but certain illnesses (heart problems, cancer, diabetes etc) rank for 100% reimbursement. In the case of the chemist, you pay the non-reimbursable proportion and the chemist collects the rest direct. If you are entitled to reimbursement of the payment you have made from a *mutuelle*, the chemist may also deal with this for you but there is no general rule about this.

Medical insurance

There are now many companies in the UK which will give you medical insurance when you are resident in France. Indeed, you may already have this cover in the UK and most companies will allow you to change to an international scheme. On the whole, you will probably do better if you stay with the company which covered you in the UK but there are a number of very important points to consider before you decide whether to stay with your existing company or to choose a new company:

* will it restrict your travel abroad?
* will it recover repatriation costs (presumably to the UK) in cases of major illness or death?
* what exclusions are there for illnesses you have had?

- are there any illnesses and/or treatments not covered?
- what level of hospital costs are covered?
- will it cover nursing at home costs?
- will it cover other members of your family?
- is there an age limit for joining the scheme?
- is there an age limit for provision of benefits?
- will the premium increase when you reach a certain age?
- is there a qualification period before the end of which you cannot claim benefits?

Take careful note of the terms on which you can get out-patient treatment under such a policy. In many cases, you may find that it is too expensive to be worth while and the best thing to do is to rely on *Sécurité Sociale* for visits to your GP and for the cost of medicines.

Provision for death

In France, all cemeteries currently in use belong to local authorities and the cost of funerals is high. However, the general arrangements are the same as in the UK. Funerals for people of various faiths do not present problems. It is best to leave all the arrangements to the undertakers but to make certain that these arrangements correspond with your wishes and not with what the undertakers think that the typical French family wants. French death certificates do not show the cause of death and this may lead to problems if the body is sent back to the UK. There are no problems about cremation except that there are not many crematoria in France and you are free to choose whether you leave your body or any organ for scientific research. You may find it useful to get in touch with SOS-HELP, which is staffed by English speakers in the Paris region (phone number (1) 47.23.80.80) to help you cope with the difficulties of a death in a foreign country.

15 French succession law

'Unlimited tins of cat food and . . . your children's larder
empty'

This quotation from *Living in France* gives a correct
description of what you may do in your Will in England if
you own only English property. If you prefer your cat to
your children, you can leave all your estate to your cat and
nothing to your children. True, your children can go to court
and in certain circumstances they may get something of what
otherwise would go to the cat, but the fact remains that in
England, you are free to dispose of your estate as you wish.
In France you are not. Certain members of your family such
as parents and children (but not spouses) have an absolute
right to inherit certain parts of your assets.

To make things simple, assume that you are a Frenchman
with a wife and a child. You would have to leave one-half of
all you own to that child. If you had two children, the
proportion would be two-thirds and if you had three or more
children, it rises to three-quarters. You would be free to deal
with the remaining balance as you wished and would not be
obliged to leave it to your widow. There are ways of 'cutting
in' a spouse but only for his or her lifetime after which the
children get all that they are entitled to.

As you might expect, if you decide to live permanently in
France you will be subject to this rule. However, you might
be surprised to know that the rule applies to your French
holiday home, even if your permanent home is in England
and you spend only a few weeks in France every year. This is

because, no matter who the owner is, because the land is in France, it is subject to French law.

However, this need not keep you from buying property in France, because if things are properly organised, there is no reason why you should not quite simply avoid the rule.

Avoiding the rule

It is possible to get round French succession rules if you are buying property jointly. When you bought your house in England, you probably bought it jointly with your husband or wife. Your solicitor will have explained to you that there are two ways of owning property jointly. One is that on your death the house passes automatically to the survivor (in English 'joint tenancy', in French '*en tontine*') and the other is that each of you own a part of the house which you can deal with separately (in English 'tenancy in common', in French '*en indivision*'.) You probably chose the former method and your solicitor would probably have been very surprised if you had chosen the other method.

In France, the same two ways of jointly owning property exist, though for quite different reasons. The French almost always use the *en indivision* method for the very reason which makes it usually disastrous for the English to do so, it does not avoid the normal French succession rules. The English should (subject to advice) always buy *en tontine* which is how they would buy in the UK and the property will pass automatically to the survivor.

It is quite impossible to say how many English husbands and wives who have not been properly advised on this point are horrified to learn that they have made the wrong choice. In fact, usually they have not made a choice at all but have signed papers prepared by a notary who assumes that English law is the same as French law and that all English couples buy jointly in the same way as French couples. Usually, it is far too late to do anything about it except at great cost. If you are buying jointly, get advice from a lawyer who knows English and French law and who, if the circumstances require, will ensure that the notary does the right thing.

It is worthwhile giving an example so that you may see how important this is. Remember also that if you are not prepared for it, the problem will arise just at the moment when one is least able to cope with it ie on the death of a husband or wife. Take the following situation, which is not unusual.

EXAMPLE

Mr and Mrs A are married. They have one child. Each has been previously married. Mr A has two children by his previous marriage and they now live with their mother who has remarried. Mrs A had one child by her previous marriage who lives with Mr and Mrs A. Some of the children are under 18 and some are older. Mr and Mrs A have bought a holiday home in France for 750,000 francs. They have bought it by the standard French method of joint ownership (*en indivision*). Mr A dies. Mrs A owns one-half of the house as her own property. Three-quarters of Mr A's half share is divided among his three children (by his existing and previous marriage) and one-quarter goes, if his Will says so, to Mrs A. At best, therefore, Mrs A has five eighths of the house and her joint owners now include children whom she may never have known and with those of whom are under 18 she can come to no arrangement.

It is true that arrangements can be made so that Mrs A can be given a life interest in her husband's share so that she would own one-half outright and one-half she can use for as long as she lives. This is, however, hardly a situation Mrs A wants to learn of for the first time on the death of her husband. She may well have assumed that because her husband's Will in England leaves everything he has to her, she now owns the whole of the house. She is mistaken, however, because French law overrides that Will.

If Mr and Mrs A had bought *en tontine* none of this would have happened. On the death of one of them, their holiday home would automatically have passed to the survivor.

It is true that this method of joint ownership may involve the payment of French inheritance tax whereas the other method might avoid it. Usually, the amounts involved are only a small price to pay to avoid the confusion caused by the imposition of the French law of succession.

16 Making a French Will

There are still a lot of people who never make a Will. Perhaps they think that making a Will is tempting fate or perhaps they think that the formalities are complicated; often they cannot make up their minds who to appoint as executors. In most countries, and certainly in England and in France, the way in which your property will be distributed if you die without leaving a Will (this is called 'dying intestate') is based on what it is assumed that you would have stated in a Will but often this is far from what you really wanted to happen.

Therefore, this is a good enough reason for making a Will in any country. But if you are going to live in France, there are special reasons not only for making a Will but also for being properly advised about whether you should make an English and a French Will or whether one or the other will do.

How many Wills?

Try to find a lawyer who is expert in both English and French law to advise you on how many Wills to make. If you cannot find one, go to your own solicitor in England, tell him what you intend to do and instruct him to get some help on French law. Here are some rough guidelines:

- You are French domiciled, ie you have left England for France with the intention of remaining there for the rest of your life. In this case, what happens to everything you own, wherever it is in the world, will be in accordance with French law. If all your assets are in France, you need make only a French Will. If you have some assets in France and some in England, ideally you should make a French Will dealing with French assets and an English Will in respect of your English assets, but your English Will will have to follow French law.

- You are English domiciled, ie you are merely buying a house or flat in France as a holiday home but will continue to live in England, as your permanent home. In this case, what will happen on your death to your house or flat in France will be according to French law, but English law will deal with everything else you own even if, for example, you have cash in a French bank or you own a French car. Ideally, the advice is the same. You should make a French Will covering French assets and an English Will covering English assets. Your English Will, if you have one Will only, however, deals with the house or flat in accordance with French law but everything else according to English law.

Why 'ideally' two Wills?

There is, in fact, no absolute need to have two Wills but in the end it will save your family a lot of time and money. The reason is that England and France have two quite different systems to deal with 'proving' Wills and it is simply not practical to try to deal with one Will in two countries at the same time.

The *réserve*

This is what the French call that part of your estate which must go to certain close members of your family (see Chapter

15). It is a complicated and, for the English, an unusual situation. It need not put you off in any way but you must get advice about it both before you buy property in France and before you make any Will either in France or in England. One more warning: the French have a transaction called *Donation entre époux* or 'gift between spouses'. This is one of the methods of 'cutting in' a surviving spouse, by giving him or her a life interest in your estate in priority to children or parents. You can do this by Will or as a 'gift' whilst you are alive. It simply does not solve the problem of children's entrenched inheritance rights but notaries, unused to English law, suggest that it does. If you and your spouse have been ill-advised so as not to buy your home jointly by the method which will ensure that all will pass to the survivor, you will need advice anyway. At that stage, if all that can be done is to 'cut in' the survivor, you do this by Will — never by *Donation entre époux*. For the British, this is a snare and a delusion and *does not* achieve what you think it does and you should seek professional advice about it.

Types of French Wills

As in England, it is not obligatory to use a lawyer to make a Will in France but, as in England, you would be sensible to do so. The lawyer who advises the French on Wills is the notary. There are three types of French Wills:

*   **The holograph Will.** This Will must be entirely in your own handwriting and signed and dated by you. It must not, like an English Will, have any witnesses or any handwriting on it other than yours. Of course, a notary or other suitable lawyer can prepare a draft and you can copy it in your own handwriting.
*   **The authentic or notarial Will.** This Will is dictated by you to a notary and your signature is then witnessed by two notaries, or by one notary and two other witnesses.
*   **The secret or mystic Will.** This is a Will written for or

by the person making it, who then signs it and places it in an envelope in the presence of two witnesses and gives it to a notary. The envelope is then inscribed by the notary to the effect that it is your Will.

In most cases, a holograph Will is sufficient but you must be careful where you keep it. Do not forget that it is not witnessed, so there is no one to prove that you ever made it. Do not put it in your French bank or your family may have trouble getting it out after your death. It is best left with a notary or other lawyer who knows you, in France or in England.

French law allows anyone who is not French to make a Will in a form which is valid according to the law of his own country and in any language he wishes. So, you may make a 'French' Will in English form with two witnesses and in English *but the contents in so far as they relate to the property subject to French law must be in accordance with French law.* On the whole, do not try to arrange this by yourself. Home-made Wills are usually a headache in your own language but when they have to be translated into French, they can become doubly a lawyer's joy.

Executors

French *exécuteurs testamentaires* are very different from English executors. In effect, there is nothing equivalent to the English executor in French law. Such powers as they have are supervisory only and last only for a year and a day from the date of death. They do not administer the estate which in England vests in them and has to be distributed by them in accordance with the terms of the Will. It is possible to vest ownership of assets other than land in *exécuteurs* for the limited period mentioned above so that they can collect in and sell or distribute such assets but so far as English owners of property in France are concerned, they need not be and

should not normally be appointed. Your family is, for
practical purposes, in the hands of the notary they choose to
deal with your estate. If ever advice was needed in the choice
of notary, here is an essential time. On the whole, solicitors
in England give priority to dealing with estates, but in
France, they tend to have other priorities.

Inheritance tax

Inheritance tax declarations (*déclarations de succession*) are
made in France usually jointly by all the people who are
beneficiaries. Assets tend to be blocked until a receipt for
paid tax can be produced so there is an advantage in dealing
with formalities as soon as possible. No interest on
inheritance tax is payable until six months after a death in
France or twelve months if the death took place outside
France. In certain circumstances which are very similar to
those in England, payment of the tax can be made by
instalments or deferred. The delays which do occur in France
on a death can cause problems if there is property to be sold.
Contracts to sell land can be entered into at an early stage,
though it is not very satisfactory to do this. No sale can of
course be completed until the land has been vested in the
beneficiary entitled to it under the Will and this cannot
happen until they have paid the inheritance tax. In fact, it is
normally possible to take all these steps together so that the
tax is paid out of the sale proceeds but this needs a bit of
organising.

Details of liability to inheritance tax are given in Chapter 8.

Final words of advice

If you have both an English and a French Will, you must
make certain that they do not overlap. You must also make

certain that if you want English assets to pay French inheritance tax, your solicitor includes the correct wording in your English Will.

If you have retained any contact with England, and particularly if you have both an English and a French Will, you must make certain that your solicitor and your legal adviser in France are both aware of what you have done. This is essential because of the different methods of charging inheritance tax in each country. In England, apart from the fact that there is no tax as between husband and wife, inheritance tax is calculated on the value of your assets less your debts and generally paid out of your assets as your executors think best.

Not only is it sensible to have one or more Wills as may be necessary but you must also keep these documents up to date as your circumstances change. An out-of-date Will can be as unsatisfactory as no Will at all, though even that may be better than a home-made attempt.

17 Letting your property

France has reintroduced a measure of control over several types of letting. The two categories which could affect you are:

1 holiday lettings
2 non-holiday lettings.

Holiday lettings

Lettings of this kind are free of all control but they must be genuine holiday lettings. This means that the letting must be:

- to a tenant who has a permanent home of his own elsewhere
- for a period which is clearly within 'the season'
- of property in a holiday area.

It follows that if you have a flat in a part of France where there is skiing, a holiday letting will be during the winter months and possibly also during the high summer for most of these areas have two seasons. If you want to make a holiday letting on the Mediterranean coast, you could do so in summer and also around Christmas or Carnival time, and if you were letting in Paris, presumably August would be the ideal month.

No one can be a 'holiday' tenant if they have no other home or if they use the premises for business. It is unlikely that tenants from outside France are there except on holiday but you must make sure that this is the case. Obviously, holiday lettings will be for short periods but the test is not the length of the letting period but the length of the holiday season where the letting takes place.

The reason for taking care in this way is that if you discover your tenant is not in fact a 'holiday' tenant, you may have difficulty in ending the tenancy since the letting may be one protected by law.

Rules of letting property

There are certain golden rules about the letting of your own home. You must never assume that anyone will behave in your flat as you would expect to behave yourself. You can try to find your own tenants. This probably means advertising in suitable newspapers or possibly by word of mouth although friends and acquaintances might be able to help. The ideal situation is to build up a list of tenants who return year after year and pass your name on to their friends.

It is wise to take a handsome deposit in advance to cover damages, electricity and phone bills and always to take rent in advance. Your rents will be liable to French income tax but, if you are not resident for tax purposes in France, it is likely that the total rent collected each year will be below the amount at which you start being liable for tax. If you plan to use a French estate agent, you should follow these guidelines:

- only use a firm which has a good personal recommendation from someone whose judgement you trust
- difficult though it may be, if you have views about the nationalities of your tenants, you must tell your agents
- you should not be charged more than about 15% commission and you should agree this with the agents at the beginning

- most agents use a standard tenancy agreement but, for very short lets, no agreement is worth much. What is essential is that the agreement states the tenant's home address and that they are using your property only for holidays
- there are some agents who retain deposit cheques and do not pay them in until the end of the tenancy or return them if they are not needed. This is absolutely improper. All rent and deposit cheques received by agents must be banked as soon as they are received
- experience and enquiry will help you to decide on the proper rent for any given period. Agents may let the property for more than you expect, then keep the balance and charge both you and the tenant commission. It is worth checking with tenants the amount of rent they were paying.

Whether you let through an agent or organise lettings yourself, you must not forget to arrange for each 'turn round'. Some agents will deal with this but others will not. It is not always easy to find someone you can trust to do this for you after each tenant leaves and before the new one arrives. In some blocks, the *gardienne* will do this for you but as most 'turn rounds' happen on Saturday afternoons or on Sundays, she may not be prepared to do this.

However good your agent may be and whatever promises have been made to you, it is foolish to expect a regular income from holiday lettings. Ideally, rents from short lettings pay for your own holidays or your outgoings for the rest of the year. You should buy property in France either for your own holidays or for a permanent home, and not because it is in a good letting area.

Long-term lettings

If you are going to be away from your home for a long time, you can let it, but you must be aware of both the law which governs the circumstances in which you can regain possession and the various other factors which affect your relationship with your tenant. There are often restrictions on the amount of rent you can charge and there are many technical requirements which you have to fulfil.

This does not mean that you should be discouraged from a long-term let. Many more people live in rented accommodation in France than in the UK and you should have no difficulty in finding a tenant. As usual, the question is, is he or she the right tenant? As bank references in France are not normally obtainable, it is acceptable for a landlord to ask a prospective tenant for their last six rent receipts and even their tax returns. The most sensible thing to do is to put yourself in the hands of a reputable firm of agents who will organise the letting for you. Lawyers are not usually involved in drawing up leases of private dwellings. Although agents will be able to complete the blanks of a standard form of lease, you must make certain before signing anything that you have understood your rights and liabilities. If you have any doubts, your local legal adviser who helped you buy the property should be able to explain everything to you.

General guidelines for letting property

1   If you are letting a flat in a condominium you are free to do so provided that your tenant behaves properly. If you are contemplating a long let, it is advisable to inform the *syndic* and you should always tell the *gardienne* if anyone other than yourself is occupying the flat: friend, relation or tenant.

2   Whether the letting is a holiday let or a long-term let, you must make sure that your tenant is aware of the rules in the *règlement de copropriété* of the condominium.

3   On a long let, you will be able to pass on to your tenant some of the service charges. You can do this by agreeing a round figure to be added to each rent payment and then

once a year giving to the tenant a copy of your service charge account to check and asking for a 'topping up' figure if necessary.

4 Do not forget to check your insurance position. You should certainly inform the insurance company of your lettings.

5 If you have a series of short lettings, make certain that each tenant complies with the internal regulations about car parking, use of the swimming-pool or other facilities and not hanging up clothes on the balcony to dry.

Chapter 11 looks at the situation more from the tenant's point of view, but it should be read in conjunction with this chapter if you are thinking of letting your property.

18 Selling your property

It is impossible to know when you buy a property how long you are going to remain in it or what will be the reasons for wanting to sell it. No one other than the expert should buy property in France purely as an investment but that does not mean to say that you should not expect its value to keep pace with inflation. If you have bought a 'new' flat, so that the stamp duty you paid was well below the usual rate, and you were the first buyer from the developer, and you sell within five years of completion of the building, your buyer will again pay a low stamp duty. With the high rates of stamp duty in France, you may think that this makes the flat cheaper and easier to sell, but this is often untrue. Since high stamp duties are payable on 'old' properties, their sale price reflects this. Alternatively, the price of a 'new' property may be increased to take account of the low stamp duties.

There is no doubt that a well-cared-for flat or house sells more easily than one which is dilapidated but you must remember that furnishing styles vary enormously from country to country. However, in general, it is advantageous to include the furnishings in the sale price. Second-hand furniture and equipment of any kind commands only the lowest possible prices in France if sold separately from a home. Therefore, it is preferable, if you do not need them elsewhere, to add something on to the sale price for kitchen equipment, such as dishwashers and refrigerators, rather than to try to sell it elsewhere.

Estate agents

Take the greatest care in your choice of estate agent as their quality can vary widely. It is preferable to choose one who is well recommended by an *independent* source. Remember that French agents tend to interest themselves in only a very small local area.

If you think that your property will be particularly attractive to the non-French, and possibly to a particular nationality, you can use an agent in England or elsewhere. For a variety of reasons, this is not to be recommended except in the case of agents who have a proved long-term practical knowledge of French methods of dealing with sales and particulars of property.

You can try to sell without the use of an agent (known as *particulier à particulier* privately) but except in a large town this is probably not a good idea. Advertisements in English Sunday newspapers do produce results and save commission but you will be very much 'on your own' if you use this method, with no one to offer you advice.

Selling commission

Estate agents' commission is not fixed by scale but is currently about 5% inclusive of TVA and is sometimes negotiable. No one may deal with the sale of property in France without a *carte professionnelle* and a written authority from the owner to act. Without this, even if a sale results, no commission is payable. Most authorities (*mandats*) give exclusive agencies for a limited period and are then renewable for further periods unless written notice of determination is given.

Be careful how the question of commission is dealt with. In most parts of France it is the seller who pays in full but you must enquire about this. Many agents suggest a selling price and then add on their commission and you sell at that higher price. You will then get the price net of commission although, of course, it is you who has the liability to pay the commission. This is not the same as buyers paying agents' commission, which except by local custom or special arrangement, they do not. (See Chapter 4.)

Commission is earned when contracts are signed. Virtually every contract states that the parties were introduced by XYZ estate agent as a result of which commission of a set amount is payable by the seller. Agents have found it necessary, in many standard forms of contract, to ask the parties to undertake that, if by mutual agreement they cancel the contract but then proceed to complete the transaction without informing the agent in the hope of avoiding the payment of commission, *both* parties will become liable to pay.

There is no reason why initially the agent should not prepare the contract but you are well-advised to have it checked by your local adviser before you sign it. In most cases, you do not need a notarial contract but if your agent produces anything other than a *compromis de vente*, make sure you have it checked. Your agent cannot properly prepare a contract without seeing the *acte de vente* to you and, if you are selling a flat, your *règlement de copropriété*. If you have not got the *expedition* of your *acte de vente* (see Chapter 4), all you need to remember is the name of the notary who acted in the purchase and the date of the purchase. He will supply you with a further copy.

Normally, if you or your local adviser had no problems with the notary who acted for you on your purchase, insert his name as acting in the sale. Do not agree to a change of notary but, if the buyer wants to use an additional notary, then this is in order and both will be involved. In any event, sellers do not pay notarial fees.

Take note of the date shown in the contract. It is very rare for both parties to sign on the same date. This is important for both seller and buyer if the buyer is getting a mortgage, since the period during which the contract is conditional on the buyer getting the loan starts from the date of the contract.

Once the contract has been signed, send it (or a copy) to your notary. Although on a sale, local advice may seem less necessary than on a purchase, this is not always so. Your local adviser will organise the paper work with the notary, but if you think you can deal with a problem yourself, go and see him yourself and do not leave this to the agent.

The tax position

If you are selling your principle private residence in France, there will be no capital gains tax liability. It is extremely unlikely that you can use this exemption unless you are normally resident in France for all purposes. There are other exemptions available for both residents and non-residents and your notary will let you know if you can benefit from them.

If you are non-resident for tax purposes in France and cannot claim any exemptions, you will be liable to capital gains tax on the sale of your property if, of course, there is a taxable gain. Such a gain is calculated by reference to the purchase price plus the cost of purchase (always allowed at 10% of the price), to the extent of any allowable work you have carried out in the house (not including painting and decorating) and to the relevant inflation factor.

EXAMPLE

		FF
Price of flat bought in 1980		500,000
Add cost of purchase		50,000
Add cost of allowable works		100,000
		650,000
Inflation factor in 1988 for house bought in 1980		
1.72 x 650,000	=	1,118,000
Sale price in 1989		950,000

Therefore, since the sale price is less than the adjusted purchase price there is no CGT payable.

If you are non-resident, when you sell your French property you are required to appoint an *agent fiscale accredité* or guarantor for the payment of CGT. This is necessary irrespective of whether there is a CGT liability or, if there is, whether it has been calculated and paid out of the proceeds of sale. This is because the French Revenue has a period of four years in which it can reopen the calculation and ask for more tax. Such a guarantor may be a French bank: it will usually block a part of the sale price for as long as its guarantee is in force and it will charge a fee. However, this situation can be avoided if you adopt the correct procedure.

Before completion of a sale, an application must be made to the tax authorities for dispensation from the appointment of an *agent fiscal accredité*. This will normally be granted if there is clearly no CGT payable or if the amount of tax calculated to be due is accepted as correct. Then the proceeds of sale, in full or after payment of CGT, can be released to you and a considerable expense avoided. It is the duty of the notary acting for you to ask for this *dispense* and you, or your attorney if you have appointed one to act on the sale, should *never* complete without checking that it has been obtained.

Completion of the sale

This is the reverse of the situation when you buy. You should note the following points:

- There is no reason why non-residents should not pay the price between themselves outside France. It is then a sale *hors vue de notaire*. Remember that if you have received the sale price in this way, you must have sufficient cash in France to be able to make the payments mentioned below, before or at completion. On the whole, there are likely to be problems in this type of sale if you or the buyer is resident in France for tax purposes.

- If you are selling property *en copropriété*, it is the duty of the notary acting for you to obtain from the *syndic* a note of the service charges due from you to the date of sale and to pay these direct to the *syndic* out of the proceeds of sale. You will be asked to confirm the figure, which you cannot do exactly because no one knows what the final service charge figure will be but you should have a rough idea. Query it if you have any doubts. Obviously, it may turn out that the amount paid to the *syndic* was too much or too little. In England, it is the task of the solicitors involved to sort this out at the end of the service charge year. It is *not* the task of the notary to do this and very frequently nothing is ever done about it. However, if works to your block have been voted at a meeting of flat owners before completion of the sale, you will be liable for this expense although it is incurred after you have sold the property. In such a case, someone will chase you for the cash in due course.
- There are special rules about insurance on a sale. They are complicated but you need not worry about them. On completion, just make certain that it is agreed that you cancel your insurance on the property. You will have to do this yourself or get your local adviser to do it for you because it is not part of the notary's duty.

It is 100% certain that your estate agent will turn up at completion with his commission account. You will be asked to authorise payment which will be made out of the proceeds of sale. If an agent has received the deposit, he may not pay himself his commission out of it and account for the balance. He must bring the full amount to the notary on completion.

Finally, you must accept that you will not get your proceeds of sale on the day of sale. How soon you will get them varies from notary to notary and depends on a number of factors but, on average, you should expect not to receive them for at least ten days. Make certain that you or your adviser checks with the notary when the payment is likely to be made and, if you are in a hurry, make certain he is aware of this. Since notaries do not keep clients' accounts in ordinary clearing banks, it seems impossible to arrange for payment to be made directly abroad. It will either be paid to your French bank account or through a French clearing bank to your account elsewhere, which will add to the delay in it reaching its correct destination.

19 The future

It is inevitable that a lot of what you have read in the preceding chapters may seem to be a series of warnings of what not to do, of things to avoid and of problems you will come up against. Do not be dismayed by this. There are a lot of things you would not be certain about if you were buying a house or a flat in the UK or trying to get planning consent to build your own house on a plot of land you had just bought. Some of the answers you need you can get for yourself because you speak the language fluently and because you know where to go to get them. The rest of your problems you would thankfully off-load on your solicitor, accountant and bank manager.

The difficulty when you buy property in France is that even if you are fluent in the language, the system simply does not provide you with advice as you go along as it does in England. Where it does give you advice, it is likely to do so on the assumption that you are French. You should therefore think of all that this book has told you not just as a series of pitfalls and difficulties but as an indication of how the French deal with property transactions. After all, there is no better way to enjoy a country than to understand its ways and no more certain way to be irritated by it than not to understand its citizens. The solution lies in trying to cope yourself with all that is involved in property transactions in France and to get from the outset proper advice from the right person.

It is obvious that anyone who owns a house in a foreign country, whether to live there permanently or only for a holiday, bought it because they were looking for a way of life different from that 'at home'. It is not likely that they will be disappointed with their choice of a home in France and it is hoped that this book will have helped in that choice. In the right parts, the climate is delightful. Almost the whole of the country is a gastronomic pasture, and if you listen to the local expert, you will drink well. France produces some of the finest dairy produce in the world and the fruit and vegetables at the local market are a joy to see and eat. As to the inhabitants of the country, Philip Holland in his book *Living in France* sums it up admirably — 'The French character is different and complex. Sometimes it delights. Sometimes it puzzles. On occasion, it can provide surprises . . . The draw to foreigners lies in France's unique combination of people, history, geography, architecture and the variety of her countryside and climate. Most of the time the French really do try to live up to their motto *Liberté, Egalité, Fraternité*, if not always to the letter at least in spirit'.

Glossary

Most of the words which are explained below appear in the text but it is sometimes useful when faced with a technical word to be able to find its meaning easily. Dictionaries always need the most careful use and technical dictionaries more than most.

Treat any translation of a French legal document with much circumspection. Never sign one, but insist on signing only its original in French. It requires immense skill to make correct translations of legal documents and a complete knowledge of two sets of laws. If you sign a translation and then give it to your professional adviser, he will almost certainly tell you that it means nothing in English. Either the French technical terms will have been mistranslated; or if a 'correct' translation into English legal terms has been achieved, these terms when applied to French legal situations will have totally different meanings. Beware also some French technical terms which do not have meanings which you would expect them to have.

Acte de vente/achat A conveyance or transfer of land. It is usually called an *acte de vente* by both buyer or seller but *acte d'achat* is likewise sometimes used

Agence commercial The local telephone Manager's office

Agence fiscal accredité (See *Plus value*)

Agence immobilière Estate agent

AR letter All recorded delivery letters in France must be also registered at some considerable expense. Many notices etc

must be sent by AR post but it is advisable to send any letter
to which you want an immediate reply to in this way.

Arrhes (See *Deposit*)

Attestation d'acquisition A notarial certificate that you have
completed the purchase of property

Bail is a lease

Banque de consignation The state bank at which notaries are
obliged to keep clients' money and which does not provide
either the client or the notary with interest

Bureau des hypothèques Strictly this is one part of the French
Land Registry, the other part being *cadastre* but loosely it
covers both

Certificat de conformité Either the certificate required by EDF
(see below) before linking up a house or flat to the electricity
supply or the certificate given to confirm that building has
been completed in accordance with a Planning Consent

Certificat d'urbanisme The reply to a planning search

Charges Service charges

Commune Local district varying from tiny village to large
town

Compensable means the clearing of a cheque

Compromis de vente Contract for sale and purchase of land

Compte à terme Deposit account

Compte courant Current account

Concierge (See *Gardien*)

Constat A report made by a Hussier (see below)

Constructible Land which is designated for building under
local planning scheme

Contract de réservation The purchase contract used for
purchase 'on plan'

Contract préliminaire A *contract de réservation* is sometimes so called

Copropriété Co-ownership, usually of land eg flats are bought *en copropriété* but also of other assets such as boats

Deposit Usually 10% of the purchase price and should be paid not to the seller's estate agent but either to the seller's notary or better to the notary to act for the buyer. If the words 'arrhes' or 'dedit' appear in the contract, seek advice since these are special types of deposits with unexpected results

Droits de succession/donation Inheritance tax/Gift tax

EDF/GDF Electricité de France/Gaz de France

Emoulements a notary's scale fee

Enregistrement Best, but not quite accurately translated as Stamp Duty

Etat des lieux Schedule of Condition or Schedule of Dilapidations depending on whether it applies to the beginning or the end of a lease

Etat futur d'achèvement Applies to a purchase 'on plan'

Eventuel means possible or probable eg *un acquéreur eventuel* means a possible buyer

Expédition The certified copy of a notarial document showing the date of its registration and the stamp duty paid

Expert comptable (Chartered) accountant

Expert foncier The French do not use surveyors as do the British to report on the state and value of property — they would use an architect. There are a few English Chartered Surveyors in France and it is worthwhile making use of them

Expertiser To value

Feuille de soins A form provided by a doctor, hospital, chemist etc covering treatment, drugs and the like recoverable in whole or part from Securité Social

FNAIM Federation nationale des Agents Immobilier. It provides a compensation fund for defaulting agents

Fonds de roulement Strictly this means 'working capital'. In connection with the management of blocks of flats, it means a kitty contributed to by all flat-owners in addition to their service charges to enable the Managing Agents to meet unexpected liabilities.

Fortune is not wealth but capital

Foyer Strictly speaking 'hearth' but technically for French tax purposes it has a rather wider meaning in that if your family sits round your hearth in France even if you are frequently absent, you may find yourself liable to French tax

Frais de notaire The *total* amount to be paid to the notary acting for the seller of property in addition to the sale price ie his scale fee, Stamp Duty, Land Registry fees and other disbursements and (in certain cases) the seller's commission. Usually, the notarial fee for the preparation of the sale document is a very small proportion of the total *frais*

France Télécom The French British Telecom

Gardien(ne) The modern name for concierge. The all important Head Porter or Portress of a block of flats

Honoraires Professional fees not calculated by scale

Hopital conventioné French National Health hospital

HT hors taxe meaning ex-VAT

Hussier Among his duties are those of a Sheriff's Officer, Bailiff and Process Server but he can be used to make reports on situations eg leaking roofs, damage to property or in other situations where proceedings are contemplated and it is desired to record evidence

Important means large (amounts)

Indivision The method of joint ownership roughly equivalent to English tenancy in common

Ligne mixte A telephone line capable of being used to make and receive calls

Location is a letting

Lotissement Most easily translated as a building estate but with legal consequences rather different from those in England

Lots (Land Registry plots) In blocks of flats or other condominiums, the non-common parts are divided into numbered lots which are used to describe the various private parts sold.

MPOA Mediterranean Property Owners Association

Maire Town Hall even if the village population numbers no more than a hundred or so

Mandat Agency agreement or Power of Attorney or generally an authority to someone to act on behalf of another

Mutuel Mutual benefit society to which it is frequently obligatory to belong

Offre d'achat/de vente An offer to buy or sell property which is not of itself a binding contract but which is often wished on buyers or sellers as a sort of 'holding' situation. Not to be accepted without independent advice

Permis de construire Planning consent

Pharmacie de garde Duty chemist

Plus value (Capital gains tax) The non-resident owner of property in France may be required on its sale to appoint an *agent fiscal accrédité* to be responsible for CGT

POS Planning Scheme

Pouvoir Mandate

Prélèvement Direct debit

Prise en charge An undertaking (usually provided by the DSS of Form E112) to be responsible for French hospital fees so that one need not pay these and recover them subsequently in the UK

Provision applies technically to the state of your bank account. A cheque *sans provision* is a cheque which your bank cannot or will not meet for lack of funds

Rejeter To 'bounce' a cheque

Réservation The deposit in a *contract de réservation* (see above). It is not a deposit 'to reserve' a property and is not normally returnable unless the seller is in default

Réservation, contract de The type of contract for the purchase of property *état d'achèvement futur* (see above) which must follow certain strict requirements

Résiliation Cancellation of a contract

SAFER A local quasi-government organisation whose duty is to ensure the proper use of agricultural land. Hence such land is often subject to a SAFER right to buy in on any sale and on many sales in the country, it is necessary to obtain the local SAFER's agreement not to exercise its powers of pre-emption. Also, many SAFERs can be subject to local politics and minor corruption

Securité sociale French National Health Scheme

Société Company but not always providing limited liability

Statuts The Memorandum of Articles of a French *société*

Syndic The Managing Agent of a *copropriété*

TTC toutes taxes comprise meaning VAT inclusive

TVA Taxe sur la valuer ajoutée meaning VAT

Tantième The proportion of the common parts of a *copropriété* owned jointly with other flat-owners by any given flat. It is the basic factor in the calculation of Service Charges and a flat-owners voting rights

Taxe d'habitation General rates levied on the occupation of property

Taxe foncière Local tax levied on the ownership of property

Testament will of which there are three types. Never try to make one without proper legal advice which is best obtained from one person expert in both English and French law

Timbre fiscal Certain documents such as applications for a *carte de séjour* carry a Revenue Stamp

Tontine The method of joint ownership roughly equivalent to English joint tenancy.

Index

Other titles in this series

Managing Your Finances	Helen Pridham
Planning Your Pension	Tony Reardon
Buying Your Home	Richard Newell
Running Your Own Business	David Williams
Tax for the Self-Employed	David Williams
Your Home in Portugal	Rosemary de Rougemont
Your Home in Spain	Per Svensson
Planning School and College Fees	Danby Bloch & Amanda Pardoe
Investing in Shares	Hugh Pym & Nick Kochan
Insurance: Are You Covered?	Mihir Bose
Leaving Your Money Wisely	Tony Foreman

Forthcoming titles include:

Financial Planning for the Over 50s	Robert Leach
Your Home in Italy	Flavia Maxwell